Interrupted...by God
Book 1

By
Doug Pacheco

Interrupted…by God by Doug Pacheco
Copyright © 2021. All rights reserved.

ALL RIGHTS RESERVED: No part of this book may be reproduced, stored, or transmitted, in any form, without the express and prior permission in writing of Pen It! Publications, LLC. This book may not be circulated in any form of binding or cover other than that in which it is currently published.

This book is licensed for your personal enjoyment only. All rights are reserved. Pen It! Publications does not grant you rights to resell or distribute this book without prior written consent of both Pen It! Publications and the copyright owner of this book. This book must not be copied, transferred, sold or distributed in any way.

Disclaimer: Neither Pen It! Publications, or our authors will be responsible for repercussions to anyone who utilizes the subject of this book for illegal, immoral or unethical use.

This is a work of fiction. The views expressed herein do not necessarily reflect that of the publisher.

This book or part thereof may not be reproduced in any form, stored in a retrieval system, or transmitted in any form by any means-electronic, mechanical, photocopy, recording or otherwise-without prior written consent of the publisher, except as provided by United States of America copyright law.

Published by Pen It! Publications, LLC in the U.S.A.
812-371-4128   www.penitpublications.com

ISBN: 978-1-954868-03-8
Edited by Dina Husseini
Cover Design by Donna Cook

"God Often Directs Our Lives…By Interrupting Our Plans."

Doug Pacheco

Table of Contents

Introduction 1
Somewhere in a Truck…God Showed Up 11
We Are Not Our Own 17
God Lives at Publix 21
Lessons from a Mouthy Tenderloin 27
The President's Own 35
Something Good is Going to Happen 39
There Was Something in the Air 45
Why We Were Made 49
Rounding Our Edges 55
Angels Unaware 59
Carnitas, Por Favor 65
The Tortilla of Life 71
Tell Them… 77
What We Have In Common 85
Last Words… 91
If You Really Love Me…*Wash the Dishes!* 97
Hidden Treasures 103
What if No One Knows Your Name? 109
The Purpose of Money 119
When God Interrupts Our Plans… 125
Curiosity Works in Our Favor 129
    On Being Selfish, Not Really Interested in Others 133
    On Being Self-Centered and Judgmental 134

On Being Unwilling to Develop True Friendships with Non-Christians 134

Alone in the Plaza... 141

Waiting at the Car Wash.. 147

How I Became Stupid... 151

My First Encounter with Mercy....................................... 157

Thanksgiving 2010.. 165

We Have to Engage…... 171

Beginning at Four Years... 175

Lunch Box Messages 179

I Almost Messed Up 183

Someone is Bringing Firewood.. 187

The Hearts of the Fathers…... 193

Searching for Family from the Garden 197

A Different Kind of Graduation 205

On That Day…When the Joy Comes 211

Introduction

I never paid attention not because of some mix-up in my brain, but I would be more engrossed in what number my favorite song occupied in the Top 40, than anything else.

Stuff began to fall apart in my life. So, I asked God a question. "Why are things falling apart?" I didn't get a response, but I knew God heard me, and He finally, had my attention.

This conversation was an eye opener for me. I had been a Pastor, a missionary and a Christian for almost 35 years. Surely, I wasn't THAT clueless!

God answered, "Well, clueless is not the word I would use, but you have been preoccupied with one singular interest for a long time."

I asked Him "What interest?"

In a somewhat, defensive way, God answered, "Yourself."

It was as if God placed a new set of prescription glasses on me. I began to look at my life, differently. I did all of the things that lots of people did, too. I was going to church, volunteered for things, and even gave ten percent of my money. I said a lot of the right things, but my focus was pretty much on me.

Then, the scripture that came to my heart was Jesus's words. "My food is to do the will of Him, who sent Me to finish His work. Do you not say, 'There are still four months until the harvest', I tell you? Lift up your eyes and look at the fields, for they are ripe for the harvest. Already, the reaper draws his wages and gathers crops for eternal life, so, that the sower and the reaper may rejoice together..."

The "lift up your eyes" part, was especially for me. Being self-centered, can be hard to see, specifically when looking at ourselves, our needs and our wants. More scripture came, like, finely aimed arrows.

"Lift up your eyes and look around. They all gather together; they come to you. As surely, as I live, declares the LORD, you will wear them all as jewelry and put them on like a bride."[1]

He said to his disciples. "The harvest is plentiful, but the workers are few. Ask the Lord of the harvest, therefore, to send out workers into His harvest."

Finally, the one I liked the least of all. "Go your ways: behold, I send you forth as lambs among wolves."

I don't know what happened next but, in my usual somewhat argumentative tone I tried to remind the Lord about my missionary service and years of salvation. There was a "click" on the other end of the phone…kind of like He hung up. He called back though and when He did, He made it clear that my "goody two shoes" routine did not impress Him.

I was reminded of all the times He had given me eyes to see people around me who didn't need a sermon, they only needed to see HIM and that I had been too occupied to realize it. People didn't need another sermon. They needed someone to demonstrate Him right there in front of them.

---

[1] Isaiah 49:18 - Ibid

I saw example after example of people who were right there next to me who were in need of a touch from Jesus but, I either considered them inconvenient or a nuisance. This is when I began to realize that I had been like an inefficient engine that spent ninety percent of its energy just to run and only had ten percent to offer.

Another scripture came to mind. "You say, 'I am rich; I have grown wealthy and need nothing.' But you do not realize that you are wretched, pitiful, poor, blind, and naked. I counsel you to buy from Me gold refined by fire so that you may become rich, white garments so that you may be clothed and your shameful nakedness not exposed, and salve to anoint your eyes so that you may see. Those I love, I rebuke and discipline. Therefore be earnest and repent."...[2]

What I have discovered; and what this series of books is all about, is that we are called to be Jesus to the world. We are His eyes and His hands and His feet. When we care enough to get out of the church and into the real world, listening with His ears, speaking with His words and going where He says to go, GOD SHOWS UP and when He shows up, He INTERRUPTS OUR PLANS.

Miracles begin to happen.

In fact, I think the miracles have been there all along, but I was just too blind and too self-centered to see the opportunity.

Since that day, many years ago, some changes have been made in my life. I pray for opportunities to use my personality and whatever gifts I have to love on people. And I am going to tell you something important.

---

[2] Revelation 3:17-19

Loving people, being there to love them, to listen to them and to give them some TIME is the best gospel you can preach.

It doesn't have to be some memorized four spiritual laws, although I'm not knocking those; but sometimes people need to see love before they can hear words. And understanding the truth, has changed my life.

****

These days, I am not your run-of-the-mill Christian.

I don't mean for that to sound like I think I am something special, I mean it like, "Don't stand too close to me if you know what's good for you."

Even though I have been a pastor; and a missionary, I have also sold cars, office partitions, pot and pans door to door opened a winery or two and probably know a little bit about a lot of things that most people don't.

And, to be perfectly honest, since the day God sat me down and gave me a talking to, pulpit ministry pales in comparison to what I have seen.

I love people, I love what makes them tick, I love listening to their speech and the way they think and articulate their thoughts.

When I sit in a restaurant, I have to watch myself that I don't become engrossed in a story that someone is telling at another table. You may consider me attention deficit challenged, but I am not. I can listen to two conversations at once and tell you what each one was about.

This book is about being aware of what God is doing around you every day. Paying attention to the opportunities that God brings your way EVERY SINGLE DAY.

Most of my life God was desperately trying to get my attention in order to love people THROUGH me. In fact, I'm surprised how easy it was for me to be so completely deaf to the needs of people at work, at the grocery store…just about everywhere!

In an article I found online at a web page called desiringgod.org, Pastor Joseph Tenny writes,

"Jesus told the story of the Good Samaritan — a man is on his way from Jerusalem to Jericho. He was robbed, stripped, beaten, and left for dead on the side of the road. Three people stop by. First, a priest. He walks by, pretends he doesn't see it, and moves along. Second, a Levite. He ignores the man (not looking good for the religious folks).

Finally, a Samaritan walks by (the "enemy" of the Jew), fixes him up, and makes sure the man is in good care. Only the Samaritan was willing to have his day interrupted. Dietrich Bonhoeffer writes in Life Together, *we must be ready to allow ourselves to be interrupted by God. God will be constantly crossing our paths and canceling our plans by sending us people with claims and petitions. We may pass them by, preoccupied with our more important tasks.*

It is a strange fact that Christians and even ministers frequently consider their work so important and urgent that they will allow nothing to disturb them. They think they are doing God a service in this, but actually they are disdaining God's "crooked yet straight path."

God has used these passages to spark conviction in my life when I find myself placing the day's plans above people, my agenda over others' "claims and petitions."

Bonhoeffer notes that the priest and Levite in the story of the Good Samaritan not only fail morally to bring aid where it is needed, but also fail to see the visible sign of the cross that God has laid in their path.

What if we learned to experience interruption differently? Rather than viewing all outside interruption as the enemy of productivity and creativity, what if we viewed our lives as communicative vessels for the sake of the other?

If we open ourselves to embrace a theology of holy interruption, we may usher in newness, revelation, life, and story to inform our work and craft and life in ways that otherwise would simply not be possible.

Now, you might wonder whether Bonhoeffer disregards "prioritization" and the practice of managing a schedule. Without priorities, nothing gets done. What about productivity? What about sermon prep? What about our daily responsibilities? Surely such things warrant stringent management of our daily routines.

After all, didn't the early church install deacons for such a reason?

Bonhoeffer's point of concern isn't so extreme. It's quite simple: The Christian's job is to listen to God and care about what God says above all else, in every moment. For the pastor, this is done in hundreds of ways, not excluding faithful exegesis and sermon prep. However, the moment we make our priority an ultimate thing, and give no allowance for God to interrupt us, we need to be careful to pause and examine ourselves.

Have we become so deluded and self-absorbed that we actually think we're being good stewards of our time? Or does the situation give cause for uninterrupted work? " Joseph Tenney, Music and Arts Pastor Church at The Cross. Desiring God October 28, 2015.

I have been a writer since around twelve to fourteen years of age and instead of trying to write an international spy thriller…I decided to blog my encounters with people and how, when I paid attention, God just showed up and did His thing!

It was amazing to me!

****

So, this book is about some of those encounters and I have found that in every one of them, I discover a new facet about God and HIS love for people. This is not a "how to" book. It is a book of miraculously unremarkable encounters from Chipotle, to Publix grocery stores.

From getting my hair cut to encounters at the places where I worked. It is a book to chronicle for you how God has awakened me to the idea that He "Interrupts" our plans in order to show up and do something miraculous.

That is what a testimony does…it tells others how God showed up and did miraculous things in the unremarkable moments of our lives. Don't think that I believe my way is the only way…it's MY way, but that isn't the point. The point is to help you along your day today…because I believe God wants to "interrupt" your day too and by doing it, you will be blessed beyond your wildest dreams.

I hope you will see, in these pages, that God shows up in grocery stores, at the gas pump, at Starbucks and while asking for directions at the convenience store. We need God to "Open our spiritual eyes" to see the opportunities when they come to us.

That description is every bit as true today as when Jesus walked the earth. People are harassed and helpless in this world. They don't know what is true and what isn't, but when they SEE the Gospel being shown in living color right in front of them, when they receive kindness from you, an encouraging word, gas for their car, blessing instead of cursing…it opens people's eyes so they can locate the true source of the water!

I see it every day!

I share these and other stories on my daily blog, unremarkablemiracles.com. They tell you about what I have encountered along my journey, and the lessons I have learned from those encounters.

It is my hope that you will subscribe to the blog and comment on what these stories convey to you, but most importantly, comment on your own experiences for the rest of us.

Lots of people wake up every day and say, "I want to do something important for God!" The whole point of the name "Unremarkable Miracles" is to demonstrate that God works in miraculous ways…EVERY DAY, in unremarkable circumstances.

If you will pay attention throughout your ordinary day, you will discover an extraordinary God doing important things in and through you during the unremarkable moments of your life because THAT is when our lives are Interrupted…by God!

"We must be ready to allow ourselves to be interrupted by God. God will be constantly crossing our paths and canceling our plans by sending us people with claims and petitions. We may pass them by, preoccupied with our more important tasks. . . . It is a strange fact that Christians and even ministers frequently consider their work so important and urgent that they will allow nothing to disturb them. They think they are doing God a service in this, but actually they are disdaining God's "crooked yet straight path." Dietrich Bonhoeffer.

"In these days God is forcefully bringing His Kingdom to the forefront of world affairs. Those willing to allow their plans to be

interrupted are the ones God will use to bust this whole generation wide open." Doug Pacheco.

Somewhere in a Truck...
God Showed Up

As an encourager, it is particularly hard when I get depressed. In fact, I have discovered the primary form of spiritual warfare, against me, is for the enemy, of my soul, to remind me, of past failures, and whispers how stupid and worthless I am.

God knows I have made some real mistakes in my life, and it became a **real stronghold** over me, especially, when I kept regretting all of the mistakes instead of healing myself and moving on.

When we hold onto something that God has told us to let go of, the enemy likes to use it against us whenever the enemy wants to.

Yesterday, was one of those days. The air was so thick I could barely breathe… It was halfway through the morning, before I finally realized that I had slipped into depression. I pulled into the parking lot of a Barnes and Noble, under a big shade tree and sat there, reminded of memories and the Father of Lies.

What a loser I was.

Ever have a day like that? A day when the clouds put their heads on the ground and the grayness seeps into your soul, and makes you want to go home, pull the sheets up over your head and hide in bed?

That was yesterday.

As I sat in my truck, of course, being an ENFP (extrovert, intuitive, feeling perceiver from the Myers-Briggs studies), I just began to weep. Most men don't act like me… They just buck up, tighten that bolt and bail that hay, but not me boy… I cry like a baby.

As I sat, under that shade tree, I was reminded of Jonah, the prophet who became depressed after being belched out of the mouth of the great fish.

I spoke to friend on the phone and spewed all of my negativity. Later, I felt bad that I had emotionally thrown up all over his shoes.. He was gracious to me and we said goodbye.

I asked the Lord, in a really pathetic voice, "What is going on?". I felt the Lord sat in the passenger seat, next to me and listened. I sensed He had that, "You've been here before Doug", look on His face. But He asked me, "What did you do the last time you got down like this?"

I didn't want to answer Him because I wanted to feel sorry for myself. I looked up, and sheepishly said, "I sang to you"!

My relationship with God is not a normal one, I think. I sense the Lord, as both a Father and a Friend. I'd picture Him with a smirk on His face, saying *"Okay, whatcha gonna do this time?"*

I don't answer Him, because, I wanted a pity party, and He simply wasn't gonna throw me one.

I started singing.

In times like these, when I am really depressed, I want to change the words of the praise song. Instead of singing the words, to the old worship song, "In my life Lord, be glorified, be glorified", I sing, "End my life Lord, here in my truck… Here in my truck".

But I didn't…

I sing simple little ditties, and old ones…

"We bring the sacrifice of praise, into the house of the Lord… Great is the Lord, and greatly to be praised."

My friend, let me tell you, I felt like each word weighed a thousand pounds trying to get them out of my mouth. That's the point of depression you see… To keep you in bondage, to depression, by focusing on yourself, instead of Jesus.

About three songs in, something happened.

As my pitiful tribute rose to the Throne of God, I began to raise my hands, and I sang louder. A tangible presence, like **something coiled around my neck loosened.** The blood began to flow, again, throughout my body…

Spiritual warfare happened and the serpent couldn't choke me, although, he tried but he couldn't do it. Just as quickly as I felt the coils loosen, I began to laugh. I laughed like a fool.

Listen, don't judge me friends, depression is a spiritual attack, and I felt those coils release my throat. It was so refreshing to see the world with hopeful eyes, again. I thanked God for setting my heart free, and I got out of my truck.

Walking into the Barnes and Noble, I went to get some coffee, because being set free from demonic oppression, and good caffeine, go hand in hand.

As I sipped my bold coffee, (with a shot of espresso and enough sugar to kill a small pony) I walked through the children's book section, looking at where my children's book would soon be shelfed, singing very softly, the same praise songs I sang in my truck. From behind a bookshelf, a young lady's head popped up. She had been sitting on the floor in between some shelves of books and I hadn't noticed her.

I continued to sing softly, still looking at books and she looked up again at me. I thought she had been reading a book to a child or something, but I was wrong.

When I came around to look at the books on her side of the bookshelves, she was sitting down with her head on her knees, and with tissues in her hand. She looked at me with tearstained eyes and just put her head back down on her knees.

"Are you okay sweetie," I asked.

She raised her eyes to me and said, "I'm sorry, I just feel so empty."

I sat down next to her, mirroring her posture. "Why do you feel that way sweetheart?" Her eyes were welling up with tears which meant I was going to be a goner soon, because I just fall to pieces when other people are crying.

"I've had another miscarriage…" her words trailed off. She had come to the children's book section, to feel close to the child she had lost. She said she had wanted to be a mother ever since she was a little girl and looked forward to holding her own child, reading to her or him… hearing her child laugh at funny stories.

Without fail, I teared up, too. I put my arm around her shoulders, like I would my own child, and hugged her. I let her cry. She leaned on my left shoulder and shook with sobs.

I did, too.

It was so much a God moment that He made sure we were undisturbed. I began to sing very low, the songs I had been singing in my truck… songs of hope and praise. She calmed. Her breathing slowed. And, she sang, too.

It was a holy moment… and, I had almost missed it. She looked at me. "My parents sang that song a long time ago!"

"Well, me too, honey, me too. It's called the 'Sacrifice of Praise'. We sing it when we don't want to, and God shows up."

She nodded.

I stood up, and, so, did she. "My mother had miscarriages, too."

I looked at her. "Look, here you stand, a product of her prayer."

She smiled a big smile and laughed. She made me laugh, too, hugged me. "I sure didn't expect this today…"

I asked where her husband was and she told me he was at work. I asked if her mother was nearby and she nodded *yes*. I told her to go and to pray with her momma.

To which she said, "I have already, but I think I need her today."

As I picked up my coffee, I walked towards the door to leave, I glanced back at the counter, where she was standing in line for coffee. She glanced towards the door, at me, placed her hand over her heart, and nodded, *thank you*.

I did the same, thanking her.

I got into my truck, and the thought came to me how the enemy of our souls wants us to *focus on ourselves* so that we will miss opportunities like this. I miss being a pastor. I miss loving on people and crying with them, rejoicing with them and all that comes with it. Over the years, I have missed more opportunities like this, but God is making up for lost time.

God loves this stuff!

Come to think of it, I never had this many encounters with people when I was a pastor…

Go figure!

We Are Not Our Own

"You don't have to understand why you go to various places in your life. It occurred to me that we are not our own...we belong to God. He places us where He needs us; He places our gifts in the settings where they will be the most useful."

I walked into a drugstore this morning to pick up some cough drops and then go on to work. As I walked into the store, there was a loud ruckus taking place at the checkout. A woman was gesturing to the people in line and was saying something to them, but they couldn't understand her because she was speaking in a foreign language.

I had already walked down to the aisle quite a distance from where the checkout was, and so, I couldn't hear what she was saying, but having made my selection between the 50 different cough remedies, I walked straight up to the front again to pay and leave.

When I got to the front, three employees, and at least five customers, were trying to figure out what the lady was saying. She seemed desperate and very frustrated that she couldn't communicate with the others what was wrong.

As I approached the counter, the woman was making a gesture like she wanted someone to go outside with her. I immediately recognized that she was speaking Portuguese. I was surprised by the fact that no one spoke Spanish in line and that no one had made an effort to follow her to the door.

Having lived in Brazil for five years, I immediately spoke up. "O que parece ser o problema Senhora?" ("What seems to be the problem Ma'am?" in Portuguese) She looked at me, and her eyes got big, and she said so fast I almost couldn't understand her! "Por favor, venha para o meu carro, há algo errado com o meu neto!" ("Please come out to my car. There is something wrong with my grandchild!")

The assistant Pharmacist and I went to her car where the woman's grandson was passed out. We tried to shake him, but we couldn't wake him up.

I asked the grandmother if he had fallen or if he had been sick, and she shook her head no. I asked her, "Is he diabetic?"

She nodded her head *yes*!

The Pharmacist went to the pharmacy to get something. At the same time, the store manager had called 911.

No sooner had we carried the child into the store, EMT's showed up. Within a few minutes, the boy was awake and hugging his grandmother. The grandmother had thought her daughter had given her grandchild his insulin and she hadn't. I walked out of the store, (without my cough drops) and just thought for a minute. I had almost stopped at a convenience store for cough drops but I was in the wrong lane to make the turn. I had decided to go up the street and pull into the drugstore.

I realized we are positioned by God, to be at places we don't plan to be. It had been almost 40 years, since I spoke Portuguese, in a daily situation, and thought it was amazing, that of all the languages someone could have spoken here in Brentwood Tennessee, this lady spoke Portuguese.

You don't have to understand why you go to various places in your life.

We belong to God. He places us where He needs us. He places our gifts in the settings where they will be the most useful. We have this illusion that we are in control of our lives, but we control absolutely NOTHING.

Not our lives. Not our circumstances. Not our future.

I had a friend who was alone after a divorce. She told me she didn't understand why her marriage ended. She had tried hard to keep it together, but after years of trying, things just fell apart. And, she felt very much alone, often asking God, "What is the reason for me being alone?"

I told her that, *God seldomly answered the Why questions,* instead, God shows us a new direction. God knows that explanations are useless. "Showing" is better than, "telling".

She counseled a group of men and women, who had gone through difficult divorces, and began a ministry to the brokenhearted and the divorced. Years later, we met again, and she smiled radiantly.

"You were right! God shows us the new direction instead of "telling" us why!"

"Trust in the Lord with all your heart, and do not lean on your understanding. In all your ways, acknowledge Him, and He will direct your path."

Proverbs 3:5 *God has not forgotten your gifts, your abilities or your talents.*

God Lives at Publix

"The entire front of the store broke into applause cashiers were ringing the cowbells they ring for special occasions. It was like a party, Ray shouted. "Let's do it again!""

My wife went to visit her parents, with her daughter and grandchildren. I stayed home, this time. I did the usual; cleaned up my dirty dishes, and did some laundry.

This afternoon, I got in the car, again, to go buy something from the store for dinner. I walked into Publix. For those who don't know Publix, it's a very nice grocery chain, in the southern U.S., at least two employees, said *hello* to me, and asked me if I needed any help finding something particular. I thanked them but said I had my list and went on my way.

Sunday's are supposed to be laid back and *easy*, according to Lionel Ritchie. But there has always been tension in the air, on Sunday's, for me. I'm not sure if it's because I know that I go to work the next day, but Sunday's always go by way too fast. I generally have a long list of things to get done.

Today shopping was one of them.

For some reason, I felt sad, and wasn't quite sure why. It was the kind of heaviness that I knew meant I needed to pray. Sometimes, God does his best talking, without saying a word.

****

When I feel this way, it's a sure sign that even if I don't have a reason to pray, God always needs someone to intercede. Anyway, I went into the store and prayed under my breath as I shopped.

People, in the South, are easy to talk to. They don't seem afraid to stop, make a comment or two, when you speak with them, and seem to know instinctively when you are making a joke.

Today was no different.

I chatted with a guy who was trying to decide between Pork Chops or spareribs. I saw him weighing the pros and cons of each, in his mind. His arms were crossed, and his hand was over his mouth, so, I modeled his stance, looked at him and I asked, "So, what's it gonna be brotha?"

He looked at me and grinned. "Which do YOU like the best?"

"You can't beat good country ribs if they are cooked on a grill."

He looked up in the air. Imagined what that would look like. "That did it for me…Country Ribs it is!" We passed each other up and down the aisle for the next 10 minutes, and each time I'd pass him, he'd give me that same big grin. People in Tennessee are sacred folk. I've fallen in love with my adopted home. Everyone is so proud to be from here, or to have a child in college, here. They are proud of the music, the biscuits and gravy, the contagious charm that makes every stranger a friend, and the readiness to help a neighbor out with anything they need.

I headed to check out. Since, I didn't have that much in my buggy (Shopping Cart), I for sure wasn't going to have anyone take my groceries out to my car for me. Publix does that you know. They stand there, bag your groceries and ask, "May I please help you out to your car with these?" They all wear a button that says: **NO TIPPING PLEASE!**

I paid for my groceries and just at that moment, my day became sacred. I had been bagging my groceries, because the girl who had been bagging, had run to do a price check. As I bagged, a very kind voice spoke over my right shoulder. "If you do that Mister, I won't have a job to do."

I looked and saw a good-looking young man, with a tag that told me his name was *Ray*.

"Hello Ray," I said, "I don't want to take your job away from you!"

He smiled big and gave me a big hug, followed by a kiss on my cheek. It made me laugh. Ray had Down Syndrome and was so proud, just SO proud he could help me. I felt as if I was the most special person in the store that day. Ray approved of my choice of bread, and said he *LOVED* the Crunchy Raisin Bran that I had bought. He said it was his FAV-O-RITE. His laugh was contagious and I started laughing, too.

Ray owned me from that moment on. The cashier looked at me, smiled and said, "Ray you are my sunshine!"

Upon hearing that, Ray broke into song. When he started singing, I sang, too. "You are my sunshine, my only sunshine…"

I looked at the people behind me, and the other cashiers, I waved my hands to sing along. They started singing.

"You make me happy when skies are gray. You'll never know dear, how much I love you…"

I couldn't sing anymore, my throat was getting choked up, but by the end, there were 30 people in 8 lines singing. "Please don't take my sunshine away!"

The entire store broke into an applause! Cashiers were ringing the cowbells; they ring for special occasions. It was like a party. Ray shouted, "Let's do it again!"

And away he went, singing.

Of course, the entire front of the store sang along.

After that, the cashier looked at Ray. "These people need to get home, Ray!"

He smiled and said, "O*kay*."

He took charge of my cart. "Where are you parked?"

"Oh Ray, I don't have that much. There are other people behind me with full carts that they probably need help with."

"Do we go this way, or that way?"

Pointing in the directions and I finally said, "Just follow me Ray."

He did.

Outside at my car, I opened the hatch and he placed my groceries inside my car. He did something that NO ONE has ever done in my 61 years of life. Ray looked at me and asked me my name.

I told him and he asked, "Doug, can I pray for you?"

There are times in life when a moment is so special that for some reason, I go deaf to all the noise around me, and my vision narrows. This was one of those times. I tried to speak but all I could do was nod my head.

Ray prayed out loud and clear. "Lord I pray for my new friend Doug and I ask for him to be your special boy and that you will love him and give him your happy smile and that he will know that he is your special boy."

Amen!

I grabbed Ray and gave him back the hug.

As he walked back, I could hear him singing, "You are my sunshine, my only sunshine."

I usually listen to music when I drive but I drove home in silence, I'd needed prayer and God sent Ray.

Lessons from a Mouthy Tenderloin

I ran out to get a few things the other day from good old Publix and ran into the store right before the rain came down in sheets. The rain was falling so hard, that it sounded like billions of tiny ball bearings were hitting the roof over our heads in the store. I looked out the front window of the store and to my amazement, there; where the parking lot had been, raged a river of water at least 8 inches deep! People were running into the store soaked in only seconds.

Of course, I had things to do, places to go, and people to see. I stared at the parking lot and then, went into what I call my "efficiency mode". This means I purposely decided to turn "off" my social people greeting, side smiling, comment making self, and got down to the REAL business of finding a pork tenderloin. It was serious work and needed my full attention. I couldn't be bothered by any distractions insomuch as pork tenderloin selection is a delicate process and is; of course, a great responsibility.

Just when I was zeroing in on a prime portion of tenderloin robbed by a butcher from a pig, I felt the brush against my right shoulder of a person reaching past me to grab my prized piece of pig! She just bumped me, said a cursory, *"excuse me"* and literally elbowed me out of the way with her left arm and started to grab my selection of swine!!!

My blood began to boil.

I placed my hand on the same selection of corpulent pork flesh as if to say, "Not so fast sister!"

The room fell silent.

The air became tense and thick with tension. Slowly, but deliberately I turned my head to the right to look the impatient patron of my Publix store directly in the eye. Everything went into slow motion…mothers of small children protected their young, the butcher on call that day, ran to the back room for protection against the impending explosion. The chill of the refrigerated section made the hair on my arms stand on end.

"I want that tenderloin!" she said sternly, not waiting her turn. "I saw it first!"

I said the same thing with equal sternness having possession of the pig but not my soul. We stared at each other, she; declaring that I was taking too long and I, asking her who made her the official timekeeper of the meat department. It was a spectacle!

I'm always the peacekeeper…you know? I always have to be the one who must "behave" and "be a good Christian!".

I rolled my eyes at God!

"Why, oh why can't I EVER mix it up with people…" *you know?*

I handed her the stupid tenderloin (I mean it folks; this is me in the FLESH I said that in my head.

"Here's your @#$% tenderloin!" and smiled like I was just kidding and she cheesed it up like, "that's a good boy, give Mama what she wants!" Inwardly, I was seething…*yeah,* and this was over a piece of pork folks! I told you in the introduction you don't want to stand too close to me! Ground might open up!

She left smiling… and inside of me, I felt as if someone had just called my sister ugly…**I wanted to throw DOWN!** This raw emotion was more volatile than the thunderstorm outside the store. I actually had to walk over to the frozen potato freezer and just tried to cool off. If you think this outburst and overreaction just a bit too immature…well, it was. And, it was something that as I shopped, God had to deal with me about. I'll let you in on the conversation, and if you find yourself judging my immaturity in the exchange, just know that your judgement is probably right, but it takes time when you are angry to quiet things down inside to learn the lesson.

In the first place, the Lord is kind…and merciful when he brings up my childishness. I felt Him kind of say, "What are you really mad about?', to which I exploded;

"Why do I always have to lose?!!!' Why do I always have to: DO THE RIGHT THING…HAVE THE RIGHT ATTITUDE…BLAH, BLAH, BLAH, BLAH, BLAH!!!"

****

I don't know about you, but when God wants to talk things over with me, I am still thirteen years old and I like to sass. It always starts out hot and God lets me slowly cool down and doesn't make thunderous, Wizard of Oz like pronouncements like, "QUIET SCARECROW!" but rather with very calm questions that are crafted to bring me back to the important things.

I've discovered the *silence of God is the most formidable discipline I have ever known*. I asked the question again…like maybe he didn't hear me or something. Again, no answer on the other end of the phone. *So, you know what I did?* I hung up the phone! I just white knuckled my shopping cart and pushed it toward the tenderloin section again and started looking at; what I was sure to be, inferior cuts of tenderloin. *(yes, dear reader…I was ticked off about a tenderloin!)*

I bent down over the refrigerator when I heard the Lord ask, again, "What are you really mad about?"

My reply was, "Well, that old bitty just stole my tenderloin, and I had to GIVE it to her because you want me to be a GOOD Christian! *I always have TO LOSE because, of course, I could send someone to hell by givin' them a little taste of their own medicine! But oh no…no I have to be everyone's DOORMAT* and get walked on in the name of "being a good Christian!"! ALWAYS! You never let me just give 'em a piece of my mind!"

Maggot filled heart, service out of necessity, not out of love…God just wanted me to hear my own heart and I DON'T EVEN LIKE PORK THAT MUCH!!!

I was mad at something that I didn't even realize. That a lot of my, so called, "good Christian" BS, was all smoke and mirrors. Just out of religious service to look good and not to be good.

****

I was a whitewashed tomb, outwardly kind but inwardly full of dead men's bones, and my mouth. Dear Lord, my mouth was just pouring out everything in my heart. I was genuinely, angry, at the very source of my life and joy, blaming Him, for my hypocrisy. I, however, did not repent at that moment. I was still very bitter about it.

Up and down the aisle I went, my attitude worse than the weather outside, and I exuded that attitude as well. I was scowling, lower lip pushed out, kind of brooding and definitely grumpy.

Two of the employees, who know me, saw me, walking. Later, they told me, "You looked mad so I didn't want to say anything to you."

This made me feel really ashamed of myself. Each time, that lady (who stole my tenderloin) came down the same aisle towards me, and each time, I had to turn my head away from her because I saw that tenderloin, in her basket. The tenderloin was from Jersey because he spoke with a Jersey accent. "Hey ya little Christian! I'm goin' home with this 90 lb. old lady, who surprisingly, kicked your butt! Ya little loser!"

I decided I'd had enough. I walked all the way to the other side of the store to get something else I needed. Of course, as the lesson master, would have it, the pushy old lady, with an elbow like a MMA sucker puncher, also decided to go over to the other side of the store.

Here, I am, in the bread aisle, and I see that mouthy little tenderloin saying, "Go ahead, reach for the Bunny Bread… I dare ya!"

I just knew the second I reached for something the old lady was going to reach for it too so I just stopped and stood behind my cart and waited for the lady and her belligerent pork butt to leave the aisle. *I can't stand a mouthy piece of pork!*

As I stood pretending to look at my phone, again the teacher, spoke in my ear, "So, what are you really mad about?" I was worn out, this time, and said, "You know Lord, you know what I am mad, about."

He said, "Yes, I know. Say it out loud, so, you can hear it."

I sighed. "I'm angry! I have to lose my life every day, and I'm angry, that I have to prefer others above myself! I'm angry, that after 40+ years, of following YOU, I am still as much of a pig, as that tenderloin!"

After my self-explosion, I left my shopping cart, right there, and went to the front door. I figured I needed the quiet privacy of truck to talk this out. But He wouldn't let me. Right in front of me, on my way out, was the little old lady. It was raining! POURING, actually. The store had three golf umbrellas sitting by the door for the employees, to help take the customers' groceries to their cars.

Remembering, the only way around the mountain, was to go through it!

I grabbed an umbrella, looked at the pork thief and said, "Come on, I'll walk you out to your car!" She thanked me. We walked her towards her car.

Yes, the thought *DID* occur to me, to get her halfway there, run back into the store, but I resisted that thought.

We loaded her groceries, and I followed her to her door to make sure she wouldn't get wet. When she drove away, I had walked back into the store, found my cart still sitting where I left it. I went to the register to pay for my groceries. At the checkout, I looked at the *'return basket'* (every register has it for people who changed their minds about something they didn't want). As she checked my groceries, across the scanner, I looked behind her, in the return basket, and there. Sitting, in as big as, life was, the tenderloin, from Jersey! Evidently, the lady didn't want it, after all, and here it was, waiting for *me*.

"Hey, ya big palooka! Here I am, I'm all yours!"

I smiled, paid the lady at the register but left the tenderloin in the return basket.

Of all the gin joints in all the world, this tenderloin was sitting at the checkout lane, that I went to. The lesson I took away had nothing to do with the lady or the tenderloin, but it had everything to do with my motives, about serving God, and others. I can pretend that what I do is for God, and for His glory, but unless we lose, REALLY lose our lives, we will never find them in service, in good deeds or in religious exercise.

We *only* really find our lives when, we lay them down, willingly. It is our choice! It's best to remember that dead men can't feel resentment. I'm going to Aldi next time!

The President's Own

On my way to work this morning I stopped at the grocery store to pick a salad for lunch and some fruit for breakfast. (I sound healthy, but my cheat days are killer!). This morning when I walked into the grocery store, I saw a man sitting on the curb, head down, reading a little booklet. I didn't pay much attention and walked in to make my purchase and leave.

Most things during my day are forgotten almost as soon as I see them. I forget the name of the check-out lady, although she was really nice and made a point to wish me a good day. I should pay attention more than I do, but this Irish setter just has too many rabbits jumping around to keep my attention on one thing too long.

The guy outside on the curb however, continued to be a thought in my head the whole time I was in the store. I immediately knew that if I was thinking that much about him that it was probably God reminding me to say something to him when I left the store, if he was still there. I said something out loud to God like, "I'm gonna be late if I talk to him…"

The Lord immediately said, "Like I don't know THAT?"

"Do you think I made you an encourager just when you want to be?"

"Do you not think I know what time it is?" I shut up…quick.

Convenience is not a part of our calling, regardless of the gift you have. It doesn't matter if you WANT to do it…it doesn't even matter if you think you CAN do it or not…just flow in your gift. The Lord has a way at kicking you in the pants and when you turn around to look and see who did it, he smiles at you and winks…

Today, I didn't get a wink. *Ouch!*

I asked God to forgive me…I get so selfish sometimes because…well, I just am. I don't mean to be, it's just I can only focus on one thing at a time and I get into this "expediting mode" where I want to be efficient but lose sight of being effective. This was one of those times…and it perturbed me that I had to interrupt my choice between a melon bowl or a fresh fruit with strawberries bowl. Why I haven't been struck down by lightning yet…I'm not sure but thank God for grace.

I walked out of the store and sure enough; he was still there. As I walked toward him, I made note that he was wearing a green tee shirt, the kind they give out as issue in the Army or Marines. Holes in the back, a tattoo on his right arm that read, "For God and Country".

Another tattoo, on his forearm read, "The Presidents Own".

I took a chance and said, "Good Morning Devil Dog!" (Designation, MARINE) he looked up at me, stood up and extended his hand to me. "thank you" he said in a soft voice. "Thank you for recognizing sir."

I asked him his name and he said it was Carl. No last name, just Carl. I asked him when he served and he told me 1964 -72…Vietnam veteran… one of 13 survivors in his company. He had done 8 years and survived one of the most horrific wars in our Nation's history. He smiled warmly. "When I finished my tour, I came back to the States and was going to marry my sweetheart, but…" he hesitated, looked down at the ground and quietly said "she'd stopped writing and", swallowed hard, "she'd already gotten married to someone else. All I had was my trumpet, and decided to re-sign, stateside this time".

Sitting next to him was a worn-out case…the kind you keep an instrument in. He continued, "I had the opportunity to audition for the United States Marine Corps Band, and I was accepted. I became first trumpet and served for another 8 years. His eyes were clear blue, his voice was now strong and proud, and he looked at me and asked me, 'May I play for you sir?"

I couldn't keep it together and nodded *yes*. He reached down and removed his trumpet and with a perfect lip and clear pitch, he played The National Anthem.

There were probably two dozen people in the parking lot. EVERY SINGLE one of them stood still, men removed their hats, and others including myself sang out loud. I couldn't sing very well because there were tears in my eyes…so did everyone else.

When he had finished, every person came up and began giving him money…I dug deep too and he probably received two hundred dollars.

He smiled at me, and said, "I had just asked the Lord to give me an opportunity to play today, then you walked up. I know my face turned red, because of my previous reluctance. He just shook my hand and said, "Thank you for the opportunity."

No sooner had he said it, then he turned with his trumpet, and began walking away. I called after him and said, "Carl, where do you live? What do you need?"

He smiled again, only bigger, "Jesus knows my needs my friend… but thank you for asking". Off he walked, singing as he went and; in that moment, I realized that it wasn't he who needed the encouragement, *it was me*.

Carl, with his thankful heart, had no room for bitterness or anger. Only a thankful spirit for a Savior who knew his needs far better than anyone else could do. What a way to start my day...

Something Good is Going to Happen

She looked at me and said, "I'm going to be fine…you're the man in front of me in line…" kind of like she hadn't noticed until that moment. I said, "Yes", and smiled at her. "Tears came into her eyes. "I treated you so badly in there…her voice trailing off through sobs. "I'm so sorry."

This last Friday I took a day off from work because of some things my partner Matt had to do. I decided to visit a friend of mine in a town not far from Brentwood, so as I gathered my things and headed toward my front door, I noticed my cell phone battery was VERY low. For some reason, I couldn't find my charger and; since it was so early in the morning, had to settle for going to a convenience store to get a generic USB cable to charge my phone.

The charger that I bought was bad. My phone would only charge up to about 3%. I turned it on and went to Google Maps, but it would take me about 10 miles before I would have to recharge it, again. This was a comical predicament. I didn't know exactly where my friend lived, and was relying on Google to get me to the address, he had given me.

As I got within a short distance from where I was supposed to turn off, my phone was once again ready to be used. I turned it on, dialed in my friends address and up came the route on my screen. As I quickly scanned the route, I noticed where I had to exit the highway and which way to turn after the exit. I also saw the three streets I would have to drive to get to his front door, but just as I saw the location of my friend's home, off went my phone.

Sometimes…I wish I had a good old Rand McNally Map in my car.

I pulled off the highway at the exit and made the left turn I remembered on my GPS. Driving to a convenience store, I was determined to get a better phone charger, and this store had a really good one. I looked for the right cable and walked to the counter. While I was there, I asked the two employees behind the counter if they could direct me to the streets that I had seen on my cell phone. The manager, a young woman of about 25 or so, said she would be happy to pull the address up on her phone and help me to my destination.

This is when the point of my story happened.

As I stood there a woman behind me made a loud "SIGH". You know, the kind of sigh that says, "Will you PLEASE hurry up!?" She mumbled, "Get a cell phone…or a LIFE dude!" I looked behind me and there stood a woman apparently on her way to work and she had stopped in for a cup of coffee and then off to work.

"I'm sorry", I said, stepping out of the line so she could make her purchase.

She grunted and with a needless sarcasm she barked back, "Yeah, so am I!" She paid for her things and I got my directions. I thanked the manager and headed out the door right behind the woman I had inconvenienced (at the convenience store)!

As I approached my car, I heard a woman scream, then curse, and with a dull "thud" she hit the concrete right next to her car. She had stepped off the curb, misjudged it, and all of her weight fell on her knees! Her coffee went flying. Both her cell phone and her cigarettes came out of her purse and were covered with coffee. She lay there moaning and crying, saying, "My knee, I think I've broken my knee!"

I came running over from my car and saw her lying face down on the parking lot. Kneeling beside her, I began asking her if she felt she could get up. I asked which knee got the brunt of the fall, I asked her if it was alright to touch her and to help her up. By this time, the two convenience store employees came out and stood there watching. The woman allowed me to help her to sit on the curb. She continued to hold her right knee. I picked up the coffee, soaked phone and dried it on my shirt and pants. I handed her, the cigarettes and phone and she just continued to cry. The employees were looking at me, the woman was crying, other people were gathering around. In a situation like this I did the only thing I knew to do…

I prayed.

Placing my hand on her knee, I prayed, "Lord, I ask in Jesus name for you to heal this knee, and to console my new friend."

That was it. No great theological statements, causing the earth to shake…just a little quiet prayer in the parking lot of a convenience store somewhere in Lebanon, Ohio. Then, it got really quiet.

The two employees asked if she wanted some ice for her leg. The woman had stopped crying. She looked up for the first time and said, "No, I'm going to be fine."

I asked her, "Would you like to try to stand up?" She nodded her head and I took her hand as she stood upright.

She looked at me and said, "I'm going to be fine…you're the man in front of me in line…" kind of like she hadn't noticed until that moment.

I said, "Yes", and smiled at her. Tears came into her eyes.

"I treated you so badly in there…" her voice trailing off through sobs. "I'm so sorry."

I asked her how her leg felt and she said it didn't hurt anymore. On my insides I was jumping up and down with delight…but I knew it wasn't due to me. *I suddenly remembered when, as a young man, someone had figuratively given me a hand off the ground…and I knew the feeling of shame and humiliation.*

I got tears in my eyes too. I said, "It's okay…don't mention it."

She said, "But, you prayed for me…and…"

I know it sounds funny…but the song came into my mind as I helped her to get into her car. It was an old, time song… "Something good is going to happen to you. Happen to you, this very day. Something good is going to happen to you. Jesus, of Nazareth is passing your way."

It reminded me of a sermon I had heard once, a long time ago.

The pastor had begun his message by saying, "It was a day, like any other day…when Jesus showed up."

I remembered when He had showed up for me and I realized His desire for me to get away with Him so we could spend some time together as the woman drove off.

He gently whispered to me, "Do you remember when I helped you up off the curb?"

I put my face in my hands and just sat there in my car... I DID remember, and my knees were all skinned up too. But like a gentle shepherd, Jesus put salve on my knee, bandaged me up, and stood me back up on my feet.

Didn't He help you? Wasn't it painful before he showed up? Have you forgotten?

I was a loud, mouthed sarcastic fool, but Jesus showed up for me. And when others need help, He will ask us to step up and do as He did. Help the fallen to walk. That's what the church is for...helping the fallen to walk toward the light. Thank God for low cell phone batteries! Another "remarkable" miracle in an unremarkable place.

There Was Something in the Air

Then he said, as if it were a revelation… "That was Him…the air was alive; it was like it had just rained…"

On Saturday, just a couple of days, ago, I visited my local place where I get my hair cut. I was looking forward to going in and getting out quickly. In fact, I had gone online and "checked in", online, just to make sure, I had a place.

When I got there a little after 10 am, the place was already packed. My favorite stylist wasn't there but I have a couple of really good back-ups so I said I would wait for her. One father with three boys all under 10 years old, came in and the place became a zoo. I like to think that I am patient, but I have to tell you, these boys were bouncing up and down on the chairs, running in and out the door and yelling at each other for petty little things…in other words, they were being *boys*.

One by one each boy was called to sit in the chair until at one peaceful, blessed moment, they were all seated. Quiet prevailed…one could hear the staccato "snip, snip" of the scissors. At this moment, a man walked into the shop and said he needed a cut. The lady checked him in and he sat down next to me. He was what I would consider "elderly".

His face shone the battle scars of 70 or 80 years in my estimation. I was surprised later to find out his real age. We began to engage in small talk, and he mentioned the weather. I said I didn't mind the drizzling rain as long as it wasn't cold. He agreed. I mentioned that the fog made the air kind of thick…like a blanket over the landscape. We sat in relative silence until he looked at me and said, "I decided to come in on my anniversary and get a haircut."

I said, "Well, congratulations…how many years?"

He smiled…looking at me out of the corner of his eye and said, "Two". I grinned big and was going to tell him I had him beat…that I had been married for 5 years…but he didn't let me finish. "I don't mean my wedding anniversary" he said. "No, two years ago, on this day, my left arm went numb, I began sweating and by the time the ambulance arrived at my home, I had not been breathing for 3 minutes… I'd had a massive heart attack."

I sat there in reverent silence, blinking at this gentleman and nodding my head up and down.

"My wife didn't really know how to perform the chest compressions and all, but she had tried her best. When I awakened, I was back in my room with tubes coming out of me. I was a human pin cushion," he said with a sober smile.

I asked him, "Can you tell me…can you tell me if you remember being dead?"

He drew a long breath and studied me. "It's interesting how you put that sir," he said slowly. "What made you ask the question THAT way? Why didn't you ask me if I had seen Jesus or a light or something?"

I told him that I really didn't have a reason…that's just the way the words came out of my mouth. To tell you the truth, I wasn't quite sure why I had asked it that way either. It was an awkward kind of question.

He smiled very broadly and introduced himself as Don. I introduced myself and we began chatting about that day two years ago.

"I felt as if I had just fallen asleep…and had all kinds of interesting dreams. I knew I was still alive, but I breathed an air that was…well, alive…the air was alive".

I asked what he meant and he told me when he breathed it in, his eyes could see better, and his senses were sharper and he could sense every single cell in his body taking in the air.

"I don't remember seeing or talking to anyone…but I knew that I was very clean, and all around me was fresh and had dimension to it…" this was no time to ask any other questions…I just sat and looked at him as he spoke.

He said, in a very matter of fact way, "You're a Christian…right?"

I nodded yes.

He smiled. "What would you call that? Was that the afterlife you think?"

Now, it was my turn to state matter of fact. "Well, Don, You're a Christian right?"

He smiled broadly and said, "Yes…I am."

"The Bible says, 'Eye has not seen, nor ear heard, neither has it entered into the heart of man all that God has prepared for those who love Him. It also says to be absent from the body is to be present with the Lord.'"

Don teared up a bit and nodded. "I learned a song years ago that Bill Gaither sang… 'Jesus, Jesus, Jesus, like the fragrance after the rain…'"

Then he said, as if it were a revelation… "That was Him…the air was alive; it was like it had just rained…" He put his head down and closed his eyes as if in prayer.

After he looked up, I said, "I would call that the grace of God, Don."

He said, "Yes, and as happy as I am to be back with my wife, I must say that it pains me just a bit not to have been able to experience more…to see more…it was so clean and fresh."

The stylist called his name, and he took my hand and said, "I'm 68… how old are you?" I told him I had just turned 61. This time he looked down at me over his glasses.

"Whatever you do, however much time you have left…tell people about the air…about the clean fresh air around Jesus."

He patted my shoulder and went to get his hair cut. I was still sitting there waiting for my turn when he was finished and walked by me on his way out.

"We'll meet again my friend."

He said putting on his jacket. We shook hands again and he got into his car and drove away. When my stylist called my name…it had been an hour since I had gotten there. I went and sat in the chair as she began to cut. I've never been one for talking much when getting my hair cut, which I suppose is odd since I'm such a big mouth everywhere else.

She finished and I thanked her. Walking out of the shop into the light drizzle, I realized how far from Heaven this world had fallen. But I look forward…to the day that I can breathe in that "living air" that Don experienced, and feel for the first time, what it is like to breathe the atmosphere of God.

Why We Were Made

"Do you ever ask God why He made you? What particular thing about you does God really love? Do you ever ponder that?"

Saturday's are a fun day for me and my wife Mary Ann. Aside from doing some home chores, we usually go to breakfast and just have fun talking and laughing about things. Today, we went to a restaurant called, "First Watch" and as usual, I went into my people watching mode.

I love watching people. I love how they interact with others; I love how they laugh and love when they are engaged in deep conversation. Now, I don't want you laughin' at me because of what I'm about to tell you but, almost every time I sit observing people, I always think to myself, "I wonder what God made that person for?"

That sounded funny to Mary Ann. She asked me, "So...do you ask God, 'God, why on earth did you make Mary Ann?'"

We laughed and I assured her that I am very happy that He made her. I explained, however, that most of the time in our lives we rarely consider how other people bring joy to God.

I mean, there are short people, tall people, skinny and not so skinny, (see what I did there?). Every single one of them was created to bring God joy and, I might add, were created to experience joy and purpose themselves. Some were made with really keen intellects, others; with amazing creativity. There are people who were created to solve problems, cultivate the soil, do heart surgery and teach children.

Do you ever ask God why He made you?

What particular thing about you does God really love? Do you ever ponder that? Even if you don't, I do. I always want to know why God made me so I can give Him joy by doing it well. Knowing and understanding the purpose for which you were created goes a long way to helping you stay on course in life. I'm a big purpose advocate.

****

Anyway, I digress once again.

We left the restaurant and went to the Farmers Market. While walking around we bought some great hibiscus plants and ferns for our patio. Someone found a ten-dollar bill on the ground and while she was asking a group if it was theirs.

I piped up and said, "If it has the picture of a dead president on it, it's mine!" Everyone laughed and my introvert wife probably wondered if they sold gags to put over my mouth.

I talk to everybody.

We left after buying some local honey (I use it instead of sugar in my coffee) and stopped to buy gas at a convenience store while on our way home. I am telling you this story just to point out that this is how God works in our lives…

He interrupts our plans!

The credit card reader on the pump didn't work, so of course, I had to walk in to pay for my gas. *Inconvenience is one of the Lord's greatest servants.* As I stood in line, a woman and her daughter were standing next to a counter doing something. I thought maybe they had bought a scratch-off ticket or something. The man in front of me was... well, he was just taking his time.

He'd reach into his pocket and not find the money he was looking for; he'd change his mind and ask for some cigarettes. He dropped coins on the ground and took his time picking them up. All this time, the lady and her daughter were still looking at something with their heads down. I peeked over and saw they were trying to pull up some kind of bank information on her phone.

The man in front of me continued to dawdle. As I said before, *inconvenience is one of God's greatest servants*...and this man was the greatest servant of all! As he stood trying to pay for the cigs, lottery tickets, trail mix, and diet orange Crush, the mother was becoming very concerned about something.

She spoke up to the girl behind the counter, "I'm trying to get this card to download on my phone, but I'm having trouble."

Her daughter was trying to be of assistance. I discovered they were two hours from home and didn't have her debit card. Finally, Mr. Dawdle was finished and as an added treat, he stepped backward and right on to my foot!

As I paid for my gas, God woke me out of my little pity party about Mr. Dawdle being so inconvenient.

"Do you wonder why I made him?" the Lord asked me.

I stated, almost out loud like a dare, *"Yes, in fact, Lord I DO wonder why you made Mr. Dawdle!"*

I said it laughing. Have you ever heard the Lord sigh? I did at that moment.

"Pay attention to what is happening with the mother and daughter..." a quiet voice spoke inside.

As I began to walk away, I realized that they didn't have enough money to buy their gas. I asked the woman, "Can I help?" She smiled kindly, and thanked me but said, she was relatively sure she would be able to download the card on her phone. If it hadn't been for Mr. Dawdle I would never have focused long enough to see outside myself. On most days, I am an Irish Setter chasing butterflies!

It is also at times like this, that God decides to answer questions we have previously asked. He chooses these times because there is no time to argue with Him.

Quietly, very patiently I heard, *"I created you to be a blessing... go be one!"* A lump came into my throat. Why does it always take me so long to catch on to what God is doing around me? I looked at the cashier and said, "Put $40 of gas in their car."

The kind woman blushed, which I felt bad about. She tried to prevent me, but the deed was done.

She and her daughter kept trying to download the card onto her phone as she said, "Please sir, you don't have to do that!"

I said the only thing I knew to say. "This is why we are put on the earth, isn't it? To help each other?"

The cashier was grinning. She said, "I was just praying God would help these ladies and in you walked!"

God had used her to pray so I would step up and serve. I'm such a big baby because I started to tear up. I smiled and turned to leave. The woman asked, "How can I thank you?"

I said, "be a blessing to someone".

I gave her my blog address and told her I'd be writing about this today. Driving home, I realized one thing God has created all of us for...to be a blessing to others. They will know we are Christians by our love...and sometimes the Lord sends Mr. Dawdle's of this world to slow us down and get our attention on His priorities instead of our own. The next time you're inconvenienced, just realize you may be getting positioned to be a blessing.

God bless Mr. Dawdle.

Rounding Our Edges

"We are all rough timber…we are all; when compared to Jesus Himself, warped versions of the beautiful timber we were destined to be."

For those who don't know, after two years, I have moved on from my tile gig and have begun…an apprenticeship of sorts, with my friend Matt. Matt builds homes, does renovations, tiles floors, (that's where I come in). He does plumbing electrical and many other things that are home improvement centered. He is really good…a master craftsman…and then… there's me.

This morning we cut base trim for a home we are finishing up. Since both of our sanders were elsewhere, I began hand sanding some of the cut pieces. Now…if I were to give an analogy of building prowess, Matt is Michelangelo, I am little Billy in first grade with his box of crayons. I may be a little better than that, but not much. I am like builder Bob with my toy hammer…Matt looks at my toolbox and tries hard to contain his laughter…He wonders why I have my rachet set on a construction framing job…but what HE doesn't know is, I was a Tenderfoot Boy Scout and I remembered our motto "Be Prepared!" for what…I'm not sure.

While sanding the base trim, (I was just supposed to knock off the splinters and any rough-cut areas… I began thinking how straight and square the edges of that trim was. *I'll bet it would look better if I sanded down and rounded those edges!*

I thought to myself. I could only imagine how proud Matt would be when he came back and saw how I had gone the extra mile. I was extremely proud of myself. Day two on the job and look at me! I would be building my own home soon I thought to myself.

Luckily, I had only finished my masterpiece on ONE of the base trim pieces. Matt…only 39 but VERY patient and wise for his age, looked at the piece and made a low guttural sound…smiled and said, "a…we don't want sanded rounded edges…base trim is supposed to be straight and flat."

I smiled, turned a little red, and said, "Oh…okay!"

It hadn't occurred to me that some wood wasn't supposed to be smoothed and rounded. And, like every writer and part time teacher…I came a-way with a lesson.

I think Immanuel Kant is credited for saying, "Out of the crooked timber of humanity, no straight thing was ever made".

In my effort to "beautify" the base trim with rounded edges, it never occurred to me that in life, God creates us with sharp edges on purpose. We are all rough timber…we are all; when compared to Jesus Himself, warped versions of the beautiful timber we were destined to be.

It is only through time, and a LOT of handling by God, by others sent by God, that the rough places are made smooth…and it usually involves some pain and lots of friction with other people. Some of our smooth edges NEVER get sanded down, because we won't submit them to the sandpaper of the Holy Spirit.

God never destined you to remain a coarse piece of lumber thrown into the lumber yard of this earth to be eaten by termites and die. He created each of us to be a vessel of honor…to be used in His house. Expensive, hand fashioned Frames, and cups and saucers, and plates. Others he created to be glorious statues which stand as testimony to His Glory.

It may seem to some of us, that we were designed to be the wooden toilet seat in the outhouse, BUT THAT ISN'T TRUE! (even if it sometimes feels true). But we don't get to decide which part of the building we are designed for…the glorious thing is, that we get to be a part of God's House at all!

It was no random decision that Jesus came into this world and became a carpenter. He knows how to choose the correct wood for the correct job. He knows where to sand and where NOT to sand. He knows how to make each of us suited for the place we are supposed to be. You are not finished yet my friend.

God has you on His work bench and is still fashioning you for His purpose on this earth. Don't jump off the work bench…he will one day be finished and you and I both will be perfect. I may not ever become a master builder like Matt, but if he doesn't kill me first, I may get good enough to have my own tape measure…

Angels Unaware

I got a talking to yesterday by a woman sitting and waiting to give blood. Here in my newly adopted home of Brentwood Tennessee, I discovered there only one location where one can donate blood but it's all the way in downtown Nashville.

I called the local Red Cross and they informed me that if I would arrive at the Cool Springs Galleria (a local mall three blocks away from our townhome,) that I could go to the rented area where the Red Cross draws blood from donors.

It made sense.

In these days of slashed price sales merchandising, it is a "knockdown, drag out" atmosphere when stores are down to their last Richard Simmons workout video or whatever the new fad is that retailers are hawking.

When a young man came out to the hallway in the mall to tell his mother that there were 10 people waiting for the limited supply of 5 particular toys, his mother told him to, "put on a helmet and some pads and get back in there!"

The young man disappeared into the sea of humanity and was never seen again. This is where blood is greatly needed…in the shopping centers.

When I arrived, I was handed some paperwork to fill out. I took my seat and began looking it over. A woman sitting next to me was doing the same thing. She was quite elderly maybe in her late 80's, and a bit gaunt. I didn't think it was a good idea for her to be donating blood, but; of course, I only play a doctor on television, so I kept quiet.

As I scanned the forms and filled in the information, the elderly woman looked up and saw me filling out my information and decided my penmanship was atrocious. She was not pleased and just began speaking. She said, "Sir, would you please look at me?"

I looked up, thinking she needed me to take her forms up to the reception area. She looked directly in my eyes and said, "When you begin forming a letter on paper sir, you should be sure each letter resembles something from the English alphabet."

I sat blinking, looking at her thinking she was making a joke, but; no, she was quite serious. She continued. "The letters of the alphabet are our greatest gift, they enable us to be free people, and express our thoughts, convey great ideas and write our music, prose and poetry."

I sat enamored with this woman. It was easy to see she had been a teacher by vocation, but more importantly, she was a teacher by gifting. It was in the fabric of her being.

When she spoke, her eyes lifted upward, her head and chin were raised, and she spoke as a true elder of our society. She was not being harsh. I was inspired aside from the fact that she had just said, cave painters knew more than I did about penmanship.

The harshness came when she then narrowed her eyelids and said, "Your handwriting is an assault on humanity!"

I looked down at my partially filled out forms. I HAD been in a hurry, and I had to admit, it was not my best offering. I looked back up at her and she smiled a kind smile. She said, "Throw those away and go get new forms, let me show you."

Aside from never having had an individual make an editorial statement about my penmanship, as a lifelong lover of letters, I thought she was exaggerating about the poor formation of my letters on the written page. Nevertheless, remembering that no one is above improvement and, that my parents had always told me to respect my elders.

I obeyed, throwing my forms into the trash and going back over to my seat.

She asked me to show her how I held my pen. I complied, and she smiled. "Good, your teachers weren't the problem…that means it is you!"

I grinned and asked, "What do you mean?"

She again squared up to me looking me in the eye and said, "If the root of a tree determines whether the tree will stand tall or lean, then how one holds their pen determines whether or not their handwriting will be legible or not!"

I thought to myself, "Surely there is a hidden camera around here and this woman is an actor." I became wary, but in all honesty, I really LIKED this lady. What she was doing was an act of humility. She was taking the chance that elders in bygone years took for granted; that her student would be respectful and listen. She had her man.

"Yes, ma'am please continue."

There was another guy around my age sitting there taking all of this in and while he clipped his fingernails, he laughed a little and said, "Heh, heh, that's right…let her teach ya how we do it!"

She rolled her eyes and realized how what she was doing was being perceived, she sat back in her chair and said, "I'm sorry, perhaps I shouldn't have said anything."

It isn't every day that someone lays down their life for me. Not currently being a member of a local church, I seldom have many people speak into my life anymore as they did in years past. That's my fault. The sting of her earnest interest in my handwriting felt…. *GOOD*.

I realized at that moment that denying our pride and allowing someone to "re-teach" us was a kindness that is unknown these days. Here was a stranger, offering her gifting to a stranger and courageously believing it was going to be received graciously.

Although, it was embarrassing and stung, I felt that water was being poured into my soul. She was loving me, giving me maybe the only Christmas gift she could give me.

I snapped my head around and looked at Goober trimming his nails and said in as thick of a sarcastic tone that I could muster, "I can certainly tell by your awesome grooming skills that you are going to teach us all how to dress for success!"

Answer a fool according to his folly, I thought.

He flipped me off, stood up and went on his way. I turned to my mentor and said, "Please continue!".

A grateful smile spread across her face and she said incredulously, "Really?!"

I replied, "Certainly, I'm hooked now!"

The nurse called her name, but she said, "let someone else go ahead of me please." She did that 6 times in the hour we sat in the main hallway of the Galleria Mall. There was a thrill in her voice as she spoke to me, showing me classic exercises for practicing my penmanship.

I felt like Hoke in "Driving Miss Daisy."

It was a lot of fun and we laughed a lot when I would make a mistake. Little by little my hand remembered how well I used to write. I remembered that discipleship is done in this way.

At one point, she placed her hand over mine while I was practicing making a perfect "O" and; for just a very brief second, I remembered my mother had done the same thing. I miss my mom. My hand began to shake and even though I tried to restrain tears, they rolled down my face. I told her I was sorry, but that she so reminded me of how my mother and teachers taught me.

She beamed, smiled and said, "I taught my son in this same way. I lost him when he was 37 to blood cancer." She finished by saying, "I donate blood in his honor".

Well, by now I was a mess. People were passing by; tears were flowing down my face and the form I had been practicing my penmanship on was tear stained. She was crying too. I told her I was so sorry for her loss and for my behavior at that moment. I said to her, "I just know that the roots of your son's tree were deep and strong. How fortunate he was to have you in his life."

I could barely get the words out. Here I was, in my construction clothes, with dirty fingernails and hands. The nurse kept calling my name, but I just looked at her and said I would have to re-schedule.

My new mentor placed the pen down, took my face in her hands and kissed my cheek. "Many men your age, have forgotten how to cry" she said, looking away and out at the crowds shopping. "To me, we owe each other as human beings the courtesy of vulnerability."

Here was a Godly woman, mentoring me, loving me, and bequeathing to a stranger perhaps something she wished she could have given to her son.

We sat there for a few minutes and I reached over and held her hand. I asked her name and to please let me know how to stay in contact. In the best penmanship I could use, I wrote my name, email, phone number, shoe size, and favorite meal… Anything I could write to make sure she could find me again. She declined to give me her information but told me her name was Vera.

"I would prefer not to if that is alright with you."

I nodded in agreement but was sad that I may not get to see her again.

At this point she stood up and walked to the receptionist and waved goodbye to me as she went in to give blood. I thought about waiting for her, but I felt that it was more respectful to give her some privacy and not hover. Before she went in to donate blood, she looked at the note I had handed her and smiled.

"Lovely penmanship darling." She walked into her appointment.

At that moment, I realized once again, the lengths that God will go to show us how much he loves us. I went to give blood and came away with a renewed soul.

It was December 5th but Christmas came early for me, this year. *God bless you, Vera… you exemplify* the scripture in Hebrews 13:2, "Do not forget to show hospitality to strangers, for by so doing some people have shown hospitality to angels without knowing it".

I've had my angelic visit for this year.

Carnitas, Por Favor

I always buy something for lunch on the days that I get off early. Today it was Chipotle. It was after 2 p.m. so there were only a few people in line. One young girl had pulled in quickly right next to me and ran in ahead of me. She seemed to be in a hurry.

When I walked into the restaurant to stand in line and order, the burrito dude behind the tortilla steamer was ticked off because there were not enough workers up on the line and the two or three people waiting for their food had no one to help put their salsa and guac on their food.

So, he yelled! "Hey! We need some help up on the line!"

One or two people looked at the front counter from inside the kitchen, then slowly, a couple of employees came out and began to help. I tried to be friendly, but today, burrito dude was angry at everyone.

He scowled at me and said, "What's yours?"

I smiled and ordered my usual, "Burrito, Carnitas white rice, black beans."

He steamed the tortilla and was really angry. I knew he couldn't be angry with me, so instead of being friendly I decided to encourage him.

"It's going to be okay," I said to him.

He stopped what he was doing and stared at me, like "What the hell do you know about me?"

Now, what happened next, I don't expect you to just swallow.

But it actually DID happen. I admit it is a very rare occurrence for me, but it wasn't the first time this has happened in my life. The small voice inside me said, "If he calls her and tells her he's sorry she will forgive him."

I didn't hear it audibly...it was the impression in my heart and in my head that he and some woman, were at odds and if he would call and apologize, she would forgive him. That was all. It became very clear to me that I had just heard what the Bible calls, a "Word of Knowledge!"

"⁸To one there is given through the Spirit a message of wisdom, to another a message of knowledge by means of the same Spirit, ⁹to another faith by the same Spirit, to another gifts of healing by that one Spirit," I Corinthians 12;8-9.

Everything is happening at normal speed. New people are ordering burritos and employees are coming out of the back to staff the front line. I had maybe 5 seconds to decide if I was going to say anything. There are times I pass on the impression because, you know, I could be wrong and I don't like looking like an idiot, especially in a restaurant where I go frequently.

But today, the impression was so strong and so bizarre, I went for it...

"Dude, if you call her and tell her you're sorry, she'll forgive you okay?!"

I smiled...but felt really embarrassed for having said that out loud. Obedience usually never falls in the comfort zone...at least mine doesn't.

Burrito Dude stopped and asked, "What do you know about it?"

I'm standing there, inside, I am saying, "Okay headquarters…need more information…. MORE INFORMATION PLEASE!!! One Adam 12 see the man at the burrito store getting the crap beat out of him!

Nothin…

I got nuthin!!!

So, I told him, "I don't know anything about it, I'm just telling you what I know. If you call her and tell her you are sorry, she WILL forgive you!"

Yes, I felt STUPID and yes, he and the three people behind me and the two in front of me along with the employees who had just shown up for salsa and burrito wrapping duty stared at me.

Overhead, Carlos Santana was singing, "Don't you worry 'bout a thing!!!!"

But I was worryin' Carlos!

And, just allow me to say that faith in that little voice is always a faith thing…and I don't always get it right so… there's that.

Checking the inner frequency again… busy signal!

"Why did I open my big stupid extrovert mouth?"

I was hanging by a string and Burrito Dude said, "She just walked out the door! I can't talk to her right now, I'm working!"

I nodded, and kept my head down, trying to avoid anything that he would throw at me. I was so worried about my phony baloney image in front of all these people that I failed to realize he had admitted he had said something to her and that she had just walked out of the restaurant.

I had heard right!!!

Hey! I was right!!!

I asked for the tomatillo salsa, sour cream, cheese and guacamole, then, got a large drink to go and really didn't know where to go after that, so I walked out the front door to my car to go home. Right outside the restaurant the young girl who had run in ahead of me was standing there with her burrito bowl upside down on the pavement. She had dropped her burrito bowl and was scooping it back off of the ground into her to go container.

I stopped to help her…she was so embarrassed and about 21 years old. I'm a dad, and a grandfather, I'm not letting a little girl like that eat that stuff off the ground.

"Leave it there and come in and let's get you another one!" she was bright red.

"Oh no, it's okay."

I said, "No. We are going to get you a burrito bowl with steak and corn salsa, sour cream, cheese and guacamole!"

She blushed, "I don't have any more money!"

I said, "I do, it's Christmas…ho, ho, ho!"

She began to laugh and then little tears trickled down her cheek. "I can't go back in; my boyfriend is mad at me and he works there!"

Now I put two and two together. *This is Burrito Dudes girlfriend!* I grabbed her hand, pulled her in behind me and marched up to Burrito Dude who was dumbfounded that I was standing there again, but this time with his girlfriend. "She dropped her burrito bowl outside on the parking lot and I'm going to buy her another one!"

Burrito Dude stood there blinking. He was as mute as a stringless guitar. His mouth fell open. "I'll tell you what", pointing to salsa dude. "You come over and make a burrito bowl for me, Burrito Dude is taking a short break."

Salsa Dude did as I asked. I looked at the girl. "Burrito Dude has something to say to you!"

He looked at me.

I gave him a "DO IT, YOU IDIOT" look.

He said, "a… Stacy, could I talk to you a minute?"

He left the back, Stacy went and sat down at a table with him and just when I dropped off the new burrito bowl…they were holding hands. I patted him on the back, winked at the girl and said, "Merry Christmas to all and to all a good night!"

Burrito Dude and Stacy were good again. they sat there staring at me as I drove away.

Evidently, God uses people for even silly things like lover's quarrels and I think, if we can accept it…this is a small step towards the next move of God on the earth.

It may seem trivial, but if you will speak up at Chipotle, He may decide to use you at other, more important times. But if you're not prepared to look foolish, He won't even try. I used to be too worried about ME when I'd hear that kind of stuff. …how about you? Stepping out in faith is scary, but after a while, you just do it because adventure is what God is all about.

The Tortilla of Life

I went to get another haircut yesterday. It is routine…every three weeks I go get a hair-cut because my hair grows really fast.

At least that's what the lady says that cuts my hair.

She is a wonderful person from Vietnam. She and her family came over to the States in the 70's when Saigon fell and the North Vietnamese took over the South. She and her family moved to California.

Every so often, when she is away visiting her ailing mother, another lady will cut my hair, but yesterday, Han gave me a big hug and said, "Dough, I haven't seen you forever!"

You just read that and thought to yourself.

"Doug misspelled his own name…"

No, I didn't…she calls me "Dough" like something you knead while making bread.

This is because on the first day we met, I was spelling my name for her to place in the system and she automatically placed the "h" behind my name because she grew up baking a lot and it was just force of habit.

It is not uncommon for me to walk into the "hair cutting place". (it isn't a barber shop, but I feel stupid saying I go to a Beauty salon for a hair-cut) and all of the ladies there will greet me with the same, "Hi Dough! Have a seat…you're next!"

In fact, one of the new ladies pulled me up in the system when I came in the other day and asked my phone number.

When she saw how Han had entered my name in the system, she made the statement, "You have an unusual name!"

I asked her if she meant my last name, "Pacheco" because that's usually the name people have trouble pronouncing.

She said, "No, but how should I pronounce your first name?"

I decided to have fun with her and two of the other women who already knew it was a typo played along with me. "Ahhh, my first name! It is pronounced 'Dough' like kneading bread."

She wrinkled her brow and said, "Oh wow…that's interesting. My parents were both Mexican bakers who escaped from Guadalajara during the Mexican Civil War and made it across the Rio Grande to Arizona".

(The Rio Grande doesn't run along the Arizona border…only Texas.)

She looked at me with incredulity.

"I didn't even know Mexico HAD a Civil War!"

Nodding confidently as she took the bait, "Oh yes…it's how Mexican food made its way into the United States…my parents and other Mexican refugees brought the recipes with them…that's why it is so big in the South Western United States!"

She was amazed!

"I just thought Mexican food places sprang up because Mexican families moved across the border and into the US and started restaurants. So your parents named you 'Dough' after the bread they baked!'"

"Tortillas!" I said quickly. "My parents made tortillas…not bread."

"Oh, of course!" she nodded, trying not to offend me.

I told her they had named me "Masa Harina" in the beginning, but they had to change my name after moving to the United States because people didn't understand what "Masa Harina" meant.

One of the other stylists couldn't take it anymore and burst out laughing. I couldn't keep it together either and finally fessed up to the new girl and apologized for having fun at her expense.

She laughed hard and said, "Boy…it's a good thing I'm not cutting your hair today!" We all laughed and I sat down to wait my turn.

Han called me over to her chair and started cutting my hair. I was listening to the conversation of the new girl with her customers. It was mostly small talk, asking what her client did for a living, what they did on their free time… just normal stuff.

In a moment where everyone seemed to be quiet and there was just the clip, clip, clipping of hair, the new girl said, "I finished my last chemo treatment in January and the cancer seems to be completely gone!" she said to her customer.

That "sick in the pit of my stomach" feeling came over me.

Had I just played a practical joke on a cancer patient?! I was beside myself for the rest of my hair cut, even Han noticed the change in me and I purposed to apologize in depth when I got out of the chair.

Finally, we were finished and I walked over to the new stylist to apologize again.

"Listen", I said in a truly sorrowful tone, "I apologize for taking the joke so far. I hope you will forgive me…I didn't know you had just gone through chemo".

She looked at me and smiled broadly. "Listen, I am SO grateful you DIDN'T know I had gone through chemo!" She patted my arm and said, "people always treat you like your made of candy glass when you tell them you've had cancer…they keep their distance…like you're contagious or something. I was just thinking to myself, how I wish other people would treat me like a regular human being like you did, instead of being so careful not to bring up the subject."

Finally, she looked at me. "Without knowing it today, you made me feel like "one of the girls" here! It was the real ice breaker that made me feel I was part of the group!"

Han came up behind us and gave her a big side hug. Brianna hugged her back.

I stood there, kind of feeling out of place. Both Brianna and Han gave me a hug and said, "You're a little ray of sunshine, today, aren't you?!"

It was my turn to give Han a hug and tell her I had no idea. She smiled and said the most profound thing I have heard in a long time.

"Some people carry hidden scars on their bodies…but the worst scars are the ones of the heart!" I agreed and Brianna nodded her head.

One of the women sitting in one of the other stylists chairs heard our conversation and said, "I am a survivor too…14 years cancer free!" Brianna scooted over and gave her a big hug, this time there were tears in Brianna's eyes. Han looked at her and said, "Yay for survivors!" Once again, another woman back from getting her hair shampooed heard the commotion and after being informed about what had happened, said proudly, "I am a survivor too…4 years this May!" Well, this time all the customers gave her a round of applause.

I finally made my way to the register. After paying for my hair cut and tipping my stylist, Han walked over to the door as I prepared to leave.

"Dough…you want me to change your name I wrote wrong in system?" I told her no, I enjoyed my celebrity status being called Dough. The smile left her face and she looked at me solemnly and said. "You know, I'm a Christian Dough. If Jesus is the Bread of Life…it's okay to be the dough. You know?!" I hugged Han again and began to tear up I said, "Thank you Han for saying that."

I didn't see where Brianna had gone but she came running out of the Mexican grocery store next door as I was backing out of the parking place and asked me to keep her in my prayers. I stopped right there and prayed for her. Before I drove away, she asked, "Can I ask you to let me know the next time you are coming?" I said I came every three weeks. She said, "Okie Dokie Dough!" then threw a bag into my lap and said, "Don't open it until you're gone…I'd be embarrassed! Okay!" Then drove away.

As I got to the stop light, I opened the bag and there, sitting on my lap was an 8 pack of corn tortillas! Jesus is the Tortilla of Life…hey, it works for me!

Tell Them...

A couple of weeks ago I was out making sales calls... working with this company that removes odors out of people's homes and cars. Not a glorious job, but something I do to rub shoulders with the public.

Because of the cavalier way in which I go about business, I was looking for a place to park in my truck in order to make some marketing calls. My truck is my office, my sometimes prayer closet, and my more than sometimes napping place.

It is a big Master Cab Ford F-150 and there are times when, I will find a shady place to park, turn on a great teaching online, turn up the A/C and stretch out to take a nap. On this day, I confess, I was thinking about doing just exactly that...but, Cody showed up.

I didn't know Cody before I had hatched my plan for a little siesta, but as I reclined my seat into "meditation" position, there was a little "tap, tap, tap" on my driver side window.

I was used to having people panhandle while I was parked. It happens. When I turned to look to my left, instead of seeing someone standing shoulder to shoulder with me, I looked down at a smaller sized 9-year-old boy with a woman by his side. I rolled the window down.

Before I could speak, Cody said loudly, "Mister, I'm Cody and this is my mom. Would you please see if you could reach my plane in those bushes? My mom can't reach up that high and I would do it, but... I can't do it..."

I smiled and looked down at Cody as he spoke. He had bright brown eyes, was smiling and confident and his mother looked at me and smiled in a shy, somewhat embarrassed way. Cody was seated in a wheelchair.

His mother, Shawna, spoke up. "I'm so sorry to disturb", she said in a lovely Australian accent. "Cody's usually a better pilot than this!"

She laughed and I was impressed that neither seemed afraid to approach a stranger.

I sat up straight and muted my audio book. "Of course, I will" I said, not looking to see where the "bushes" were that held the plane.

I introduced myself and got out of my truck and locked the door. Cody explained he and his mom came to the park a lot to fly his plane…a small radio, controlled plane and helicopter he had gotten for his birthday two months earlier. His mother pointed at the tall bushes that were more like tall ornamental grass…but they were surrounded by low bushes and landscape boulders.

I gladly struggled over the boulders, over the bushes and ventured into the grassy forest to get the plane that was stuck in the middle of one of the grass plants. I recalled the days of my youth as a gymnast when I would have bounded over those boulders, but that was 42 years ago…things have changed a bit at 61…no bounding!

As I emerged with the plane, Cody, forgetting that pulling the trigger on the controls would turn the propeller the plane, he pushed the trigger and the plane sprang out of my hand and into the air. He laughed and his mother told him to be careful. I climbed back over the big rocks and started on my way back to my truck and Shawna spoke up.

"Cody was born with Spina Bifida…and he is our only child…my husband and me."

I had heard of Spina Bifida but wasn't exactly sure what it meant as far as treatment and/or healing of the condition. She saw my mind was going through the mental process of trying to formulate questions when she generously offered, "Do you know what that is?" I explained I had heard of it.

"Cody will be an independent person, but may always need his wheelchair…his treatment was started a little late."

She explained that circumstances had prevented them from getting the kind of early treatment Cody had needed. I had understood it to be financial circumstances. It certainly was evident that her son was the apple of her eye. I asked about her family and about their spiritual lives. Listen, if someone is going to be bold enough to ask a stranger to climb over a bunch of rocks and bushes to get a toy airplane, I feel an equal amount of boldness is my due….so, there.

"Have you asked for prayer for Cody's condition?" Shawna looked annoyed when I asked that.

"Thank you for your help." She said trying to get rid of me. I persisted.

"Shawna, I asked if you have asked for prayer for Cody's condition?" Her lips pursed together as her eyes narrowed. She became terse with her reply. "I appreciate your help…but that is a private matter!"

I am an easygoing dude. I never push people, always try to be courteous and kind to people and you are going to think I was a real jerk, but this time I was not going to retreat because her fear was turned to anger. I responded.

"Okay, it's between you and God…but I hope you aren't angry at God for Cody's condition…have a good day!" I began walking away.

And this is when this little Australian lady became a bulldog. "Oh…it's not God's fault isn't it? Oh…okay, now you opened your mouth so I don't care now that you got his #$%@ airplane out of the bushes…God did this to my son and if he didn't, he sure as hell didn't do anything to stop it!"

Her cheeks were flushed red and her eyes scowled at me. If you're going to try to get to the root of someone's issues, you'd better be ready for both barrels. In the back of my mind I heard the words…"this time you went too far!" She continued. "I'll bet you haven't had any hardship in YOUR life, have you? I'll bet your nice tidy life is just perfect like your God designed it…I guess God just needed a target and chose my little boy for it!"

Tears were coming down her face…and I have to admit, it had been a while since I had encountered something like that. I just froze in my tracks and inadvertently looked for a fast path to my truck.

I hesitated between getting back into my truck and driving away or saying something that would make a difference. Only problem was; at that moment, there were no words and none on the horizon. My personality type doesn't like silence…we like to fill empty embarrassing gaps with talk but absolutely nothing was coming to my mouth to say.

I could tell that my silence was somewhat satisfying for her.

She asked if the, "Cat got your tongue?"

I stood still and was looking down at the ground. Here is what I figured. I figured that pulling into this park was not something I had planned, I also considered that it was a one in ten million chance that a boy in a wheelchair would come tapping on my window. After thinking these things, I knew I was supposed to be the one here at this moment but was inwardly ashamed that I had nothing to say. No big dramatic, "parting of the water" statement…

I mean…

NOTHING. So, I stood still looking at the ground.

She crossed her arms and I think began to feel embarrassed she had been so cross with a stranger. She sighed out loud and said, "Look, I'm sorry, I am really not mad at you. You've been very kind…" that was all. I felt I should try to defuse the silence with a nice, "It's okay…no problem…" but I didn't. Again, I stood there like a cigar store Indian…wooden and silent.

As she began to walk away, finally my mind came online again and I finally spoke without qualifying the words…

"My son just discovered this week he has a tumor in his head and I still believe." She stopped and looked at me.

"What?" she asked, "What did you say?"

I answered a bit louder, "My son who is 34 years old just discovered he has a tumor at the base of his skull and I still believe God is in charge."

Shawna took a couple of steps back toward me… "Why? Why do you still believe?"

I said, "He's a cop with three boys, one of them the age of Cody…and he has a gorgeous wife. He's my youngest son, and it is wrapped around his carotid artery and nerves that could leave him without a voice. I believe because I know the character of God…he has always been faithful to me. Even if I don't get the result I pray for, God is a God of faithfulness and life."

She shook her head no, like nothing I said would even matter. I didn't have anything else I could do but do the one thing that I figured would rile her up again, which; is what I signed up for when I told Jesus I would follow him. In my head I heard the words of the song by Andre Crouch and the disciples… "Tell them" God always uses music with me…

"Tell them even if they don't believe you. Just tell them even if they don't receive you. Oh, tell them for me tell them for me please, please, tell them for me…tell them that I love them. And I came to let them know."

So, I told her… "Shawna, I am going to leave, and you can ponder why you're so angry with God, but I would like to pray for you."

She just stood there.

I knew better than to place my hand on a strange lady, so I just prayed out loud. "Father, I pray that Shawna would know that you are a good and loving father…not one that would walk out on us and leave us to fend for ourselves. Not a father that would only show us love when life was perfect. Help Shawna to know that You love Cody and that if she will only believe, and leave the results in your hands, she will see your goodness in this life. Please let her know you love her. In Jesus name, Amen."

I thanked her for letting me pray and walked back to my truck. I heard her calling Cody as I approached the truck. I started it up and drove to the end of the parking lot to make a U-turn and on my way back, Cody and his electric wheelchair sat near where I had been parked waving. I stopped and rolled down my window. His mother was walking quickly up behind him as he spoke to me. "Thanks so much!" she said smiling broadly.

"Thanks for getting my plane!"

I told him he was welcome, and I said, "God bless you Cody."

That is when the boy with spina bifida looked at me. "God bless you too," his mother had arrived by that time and looked down at him as I began to drive away.

She asked, "What did you say to him?"

Cody said, "I said, God Bless you!"

Shawna looked up at me with a tear in her eye. "Out of the mouths of babes, God has reserved praise for himself."

Cody took her hand. "Don't cry momma, everything's under control!"

What We Have In Common...

Standing in line for coffee, a man is in obvious discomfort. He continues to rub his lower back and left leg. I tapped him on the shoulder and he turned around.

I asked, "Lower back pain and sciatica?"

He looked surprised, smiled and said, "Yes! Exactly! Are you a physical therapist or doctor?"

I laugh and said, "Fellow sufferer!"

He laughed and we began a conversation that ended with discovering we were both gymnasts in high school and he and his wife are going through a divorce. We both grabbed our coffee and stood talking about our divorces and he let me pray for him and his family. His name was Saul, and he lived nearby…maybe we can get together?

Standing at a gas pump, I looked around at other cars while my car was filling and saw a young lady in a nice skirt and blouse and meticulous nails, fidgeting with the gas pump trying not to smell like gas.

I went over to her and said, "Girl, you look too nice to pump that gas…may I help you?"

Since I am an old codger, she relaxed and said, "Thank you so much…I am going to an interview and don't want to smell like gas!" I told her I get it. She stood and talked to me while I filled her car.

"You look like John Larroquette from Night Court!" she said.

I laughed and said, "That's better than Bill Clinton!"

She laughed and asked if people really thought I looked like Bill Clinton. I told her, only the ones that are nearsighted. I asked what kind of job she was going to interview for and she told me as an attorney for a local law firm. She had Indiana plates and I told her I am from Columbus Indiana. She smiled big and said she was from Bloomington!

She had driven down the night before and stayed at a local hotel so she could be fresh for the interview that her Dean had arranged for her. We exchanged memories of I.U. and as I begin to leave, I asked her if she was nervous. She said yes. I asked if I could pray for her and she jumped at the chance to get prayer.

She said, "Thank you so much!" and gave me a little hug.

I said, "God bless you sweetie."

Before she started her car, she rolled down the window and said, "My grandmother said she would be praying for me…I guess you're proof that God is listening."

I would sure like to know how her interview went.

****

At the Waffle House where I always go for breakfast, the cooks and the waitresses all know me. Mandie who has a nametag that says, 'Mandolyn', shouts, "Doug's here!"

Her arms have really gorgeous sleeves (tattoos on the lower forearms) and neck ink that she said was, "Worse pain than having my son!"

Rhonda, who has a nametag with all capital letters that says RHONDA but above it has "Help Me" in really small letters feigns a groan and says, "Not him again!"

LaToya, who has the most beautiful braids, in her hair, started laughing. "Oh it's gonna be a good day!"

I looked at RHONDA, "Just for that, I'm sittin' in LaToya's section today!"

RHONDA came around the counter and gave me a big side hug.

She whispered, "My grandson just got his cast off!"

I high five her. Her grandson broke both of the bones in his lower leg when; in a freak accident, the diving board hit his leg while he was diving too close to it. He had gotten a lung full of water, but was okay and after two surgeries, his cast was coming off today.

Mandie asked, "The usual?"

I smiled and said, "Y*es*."

This means, a large Orange juice, water AND coffee along with three eggs, over medium, a T bone, hashed browns diced, chunked, smothered, covered and capped, and two orders of toast. (It's the only meal I eat all day so…cut me some slack).

Ray, the cook looks over his shoulder at me, smiled and said, "I saw you comin'…I already have the steak ready!"

I laughed, "Wow what service!"

Before I left, I asked them all how I can pray for them today. They always give me a prayer request…

ALWAYS.

****

I bring this up because, you will notice I did not ask any of them to come to my church. Jesus doesn't tell me to ask them to come to my church. In fact, LaToya is Jehovah's witness, and instead of getting into some useless debate about what I think about her church, I get the most prayer requests from her. Notice I do not ask them if they are saved. Jesus did not tell me to ask them if they were saved. He simply told me to tell them about Him.

To make disciples and to walk in a manner worthy of the Gospel. "He has shown you oh man what is good, and what does the Lord require of you, but to do justly, love mercy and walk humbly with your God." Micah 6:8

What I have in common with people in the world is my fallenness. We are all fallen, fallible and finite. (I call these the three "F" words I can say.)

To have this in common with people is my greatest ally. Because as I walk in this world, people don't talk about "holiness" or the "favor of God".

They don't converse about how to walk in, faith and purity. They don't center their conversations around end time eschatology, whether they are pre-tribulation, mid-tribulation, post-tribulation or pan-tribulation rapture…that is stuff and nonsense to them.

Those are the very reasons they stay home on Sunday and watch Oprah. They talk about what is going on in their lives…what matters to THEM. And, they ACTUALLY believe that God cares about their work interviews, their grandchildren and healing their divorces. The last thing they need or want for that matter is some perfect smelling, clean fingernailed dandy to walk in and tell them how much better THEIR lives are since they found Jesus.

What they want…is to have someone to understand their fears, and to listen to them and what hurts so deeply.

I gave up a long time ago trying to use some method or system to memorize in order to "share my faith".

What does that mean when YOU hear it?

"Share your faith". Quite frankly, it's gobbledy gook to me. It's religious speak for "telling people about Jesus".

I don't look down on anyone who uses those methods or systems, but I'm here to tell you there's a better way. No…it isn't MY way, it's the complete opposite, it's YOUR way. Telling and showing Jesus with your perfect personality and style. Making friends with the world doesn't mean we are worldly…

The Bible says that *"…the common man heard him gladly."* Mark 12:37.

I was once in a bar down in College Station Texas (yes…I said a bar…) with a friend of mine who is a pastor in Houston. (This is where I am going to lose some of you so if you want to stop reading here and believe I am a perfect specimen of a Christian please consider this post finished…for the realists among you…read on).

This pastoral friend of mine and I were sitting in a bar with all college students around us. We were both discussing things about God, the Church and I don't remember the rest.

This young guy hears us talking about church, in a bar and believe it or not he says, "that is so cool…you guys are Christians?"

I am not advising you to do what we were doing, because it isn't to prove how FREE I am, but to tell you, that I am not afraid of the world infiltrating my soul…Jesus is my rock…but this is HIS world.

We said, "Yes we are!"

We engaged him in conversation, and, if my is reading this, correct me if I am wrong, but we prayed with that guy and he accepted Jesus right there in a sports bar.

****

In 1989 a film came out to critical acclaim called, *Field of Dreams*. In it, Ray Kinsella, sells off a large swath of his farm in order to build a baseball field because he had heard a voice tell him, "If you build it…they will come".

By the end of the movie, during the closing credits you see cars backed up for miles and miles waiting to get into that field, because it was said it would remind them of special times and make them feel that they were at home. I'm here to tell you, with respect to the world around us, if you will build on every opportunity that God brings in front of you, THEY WILL COME.

They won't even know why they are coming except maybe for the fact that they saw in you; a fellow fallen human, someone who seemed to have found the field that God has built to bring us all home.

They will come because you loved them as Jesus loved them…right where they are, but you didn't leave them that way. You left behind the aroma of Jesus and they will follow that scent to the Throne of the King. Peace.

Last Words...

I have been reading about the last words of famous people. You know, the older I get the more I actually look forward to going home. I'm not trying to leave early though. I figure when it's time, it's time. There are many who have done things of note in their lifetimes and, their last words are both interesting and important.

I have read about famous last words of Presidents and Mafia bosses, (which, don't confuse the two although there are some very close comparisons), and people of faith and those who were atheists.

All of their last words are important. What we choose to say at the moment of our death may not be a summation of our lives, because some of us have surprise endings, accidents. But for those who were dying and knew it, some of them said some very profound things.

According to Steve Jobs' sister Mona, the Apple founder's last words were, "Oh wow. Oh wow. Oh wow."

Emily Dickinson, America's most celebrated poet's last words were, "I must go in, for the fog is rising."

When I read those things, I often try to imagine what they saw. There is no doubt that the veil between life and death is exceedingly thin...less than a breath in my estimation. I wonder in my heart if Steve saw something so incredibly beyond anything he could imagine that the computer genius was reduced to his child like wonder statement… "Wow."

There are humorous ones.

Charles Gussman was a writer and TV announcer, who wrote the pilot episode of *Days of Our Lives*, among other shows. As he became ill, he said he wanted his last words to be memorable. When his daughter reminded him of this, he gently removed his oxygen mask and whispered: "And now for a final word from our sponsor—."

When Groucho Marx was dying, he let out one last quip: "This is no way to live!"

Donald O'Connor was a singer, dancer, and actor. He also hosted the Academy Awards in 1954. O'Connor died at age 78 with his family gathered around him. He joked, "I'd like to thank the Academy for my lifetime achievement award that I will eventually get."

He still hasn't gotten one.

I found that some of them were particularly poignant.

****

Billy Graham's daughter Anne Lotz says that his last words were for her 11-year-old granddaughter. Lotz's family surrounded Graham during her final visit with him, and she said her 11-year-old granddaughter told him she loved him as the family was leaving. Graham answered back, "I love you." Those were his last words.

Football coach Vince Lombardi died of cancer in 1970. As he died, Lombardi turned to his wife Marie and said, "Happy anniversary. I love you."

O.O. McIntyre was an American reporter. He died at age 53, and spoke his last words to his wife Maybelle: "Snooks, will you please turn this way. I like to look at your face."

When he was 57, Edward R. Murrow died while patting his wife's hand. He said, "Well, Jan, we were lucky at that."

John Wayne died at age 72 in L.A. He turned to his wife and said, "Of course I know who you are. You're my girl. I love you."

Humphrey Bogart's wife Lauren Bacall had to leave the house to pick up their kids. Bogart said, "Goodbye, kid. Hurry back." Not quite, "Here's looking at you, kid," but close.

****

While I am both healthy and happy at this moment, I can think of nothing quite so peaceful and wonderful to gaze upon; before I leave this earth, as the face of my wonderful wife Mary Ann. I hope it will be so, but God knows.

Don't start thinking I've been diagnosed with some kind of fatal disease. I have not. But what people say at the last few minutes of life can be a window into what is most important to them.

Like John Adams, who lay dying on the 4th of July 1826: "Thomas Jefferson--still survives". John Adams, US President, d. July 4, 1826. *(Actually, Jefferson had died earlier that same day.)*

"See in what peace a Christian can die." Joseph Addison, writer, d. June 17, 1719."

"Now comes the mystery'. Henry Ward Beecher, evangelist, d. March 8, 1887."

"It is very beautiful over there." Thomas Alva Edison, inventor, d. October 18, 1931."

****

I have lived my life in such a way, that as far back as I can remember, I've always looked forward to seeing the green valley that I believe God has promised me. As a child I asked my mother what I would see when I died. It was a curious question for such a young child.

She sat at the edge of her 4-year-old child's bed and stared at me. I remember she looked out the window in my bedroom and; at that moment, she heard the train passing through town over 4 miles away.

She looked back at me with soft tears in her eyes and smiled gently. "Doug, when you are ready to go to heaven, you will hear the gentle call of the heavenly train whistle and there will be a seat, with a quilt on it to keep you warm. I will be waiting on board saving your seat next to me."

I smiled and would ask her to repeat that story from time to time as I grew up.

As my mother grew older, after my father had passed away, we would talk often of heaven and I could tell my mother was so looking forward to "boarding the train for home".

In her last year of life, as she slowly approached the end, she would sleep often, and at least one night, as I sat by her bed in her little apartment, she would say,

"Doug, I think the train is getting closer…" this time it was my turn to weep quietly. I held her hand until she drifted off to sleep.

In her final days, I was busy at the winery, but I went to sit in her room at the Hospice. She had been asleep for 4 days straight, and they didn't expect her to wake up. It was on this day, that I sat by her bed holding her hand and singing "I come to the Garden alone", her favorite hymn.

As time passed, I stood and had to leave her.

"Mom" I said quietly, "I have to go to work, but I'll be back tomorrow…I love you."

This was when; for the first time in 4 days, she awoke fully and spoke to me with a full voice. "Doug, your Dad said, 'Come Home'!"

Standing in that room I was sure, just sure, I heard a train whistle from downtown. I choked on my response. "Mom, you do what Dad wants you to do."

Her eyes smiled at me and she went back to sleep. The next morning, February 14, 2014 just 9 days shy of her 90th birthday, my mother boarded the train alongside my dad…her had called her home on Valentine's Day and had come to the station to meet her with a quilt on her seat to keep his sweetheart warm.

What I want is for you, my friend, to know in your heart of hearts that you have your ticket securely in your hand. I want you there…with me, in my green valley. It's lovely there…the flowers make music and there are levels…so many levels in that place where you can visit.

I will be there waiting for you on the train to accompany you if you'd like. I'll have a quilt sitting in your seat to put around your legs for the journey. We'll sit and laugh and talk and watch the lovely scenery pass us by until we arrive at the station where everyone we know will be waiting for us.

****

There will be my wine…the perfected wine I finally have made from perfectly sugared grapes and my dogs will all be there to greet you…yours too! And there will be no strangers there…only friends, dear friends and family.

Whatever you held dear, and whatever memory that comforted you, will be real and waiting for you. I don't know what my last words on this earth will be, but one thing is for sure…it will be a blessing, a prayer or thanksgiving for having had the privilege of being born on God's earth.

If I survive my wife, we will hold hands and I will sing to her, kiss her forehead and listen for her last words. If not, she will be there holding my hand and I will be looking into her eyes and the eyes of my children and grandchildren.

But until then, there is work to be done, and a kingdom to proclaim…and the train is quickly approaching the station.

If You Really Love Me... Wash the Dishes!

I hear a lot of things while I'm out and about in the public square. I hear good things, like the sister saying to her brother at a pizza restaurant, "you play soccer better than anyone I've ever seen!"

To which her brother gave her a hug...they were about 8 years old. I hear bad things too. Walking passed a window at an apartment complex hearing a woman and man yelling at each other because he said she was spending too much time with her supervisor...she said, "at least he pays attention to me!" continued yelling, hurtful things said and then a door slamming.

I heard a man praying once. I was sitting in a Baskin Robbins, eating two dips of "Death by Chocolate" when I heard the guy at the next table. I thought he was talking on his phone, but ...no phone in his hand! I try not to eavesdrop, but...you know, come on; I wanted to know what he was saying and to whom! *(You would too...admit it!)*

When I finally DID hear what he was saying, he was praying for his mother...asking the Lord to give her a chance to know Jesus. I felt as if I had invaded the holiest time of all, and I repented for it. Curiosity in my case, most certainly could get me in trouble if I am not careful!

Perhaps one of the most intriguing things I have heard, hit me like a ton of bricks and I'll explain why.

But first, you need to understand how the Lord made me…because without that, you will think I think I'm a "really nosy dude"! I used to not pay attention like I do now because I was ignoring how the Lord had made me. He actually gave me the ability to be aware of my surroundings in a "hyper-sensitive" way. It is nothing I trained for or that I have learned…it was given to me…by a God who needs ears on the ground.

I'm convinced the Lord made me to be an ENFP, which is the Myers-Briggs definition for the type of personality I have. I see it is pretty much right on the mark.

How ENFP's Think

"Throughout their lives, ENFPs are always on the lookout for deeper hidden meaning. This personality type is absolutely certain that what we observe and experience only scratches the surface of reality. ENFPs don't believe in coincidence because they know that we are all interconnected, and they know that everything we do has an impact on the world around us. It isn't enough for ENFPs to just observe and collect data; they need to put it into the proper context, and they believe speculative, abstract thinking helps them to do so.

ENFPs make a great effort to keep their eyes open and their minds alert, and their strong observational abilities frequently combine with their active minds to bring on those "a-ha!" moments exactly when they are needed. ENFPs experience these leaps of understanding as creative bursts, and they are very enthusiastic about translating those bursts into real-life activity."

I include this so you will understand that it is written onto my soul, to always be observing and listening to things going on around me. If it looks like I'm nosy…well, maybe I am…but I'm not trying to be rude, I'm trying to understand the STORY, because the story is EVERYTHING! God is speaking in EVERY SINGLE THING around us.

So, back to the thing I heard the other day. I was at Sonic, the highly health unconscious drive in of gastronomic delights…sipping on a 44oz Hwy 44 Frozen Limeade. I was listening to a message on my phone through my Bluetooth speakers in my truck. As I sat there listening to the message, the couple in the car right next to me were having a discussion.

I put the phone message on "hold".

The woman was saying something to her husband about their relationship. They could not see my window was down because of the gigantic menus the size of a drive-in movie screen that separate our cars, so they didn't lower their voices. She began,

"You keep asking me if I'm happy in our marriage…and for the most part…if you want me to answer honestly, Yes, I am." Her husband, probed deeper asking "for the most part?" (which; in my opinion, was sort of like leaning into a right hook…brave man.)

She sat quietly. "You always SAY, 'I love you so much!' You're a really great dad…and when you say those things, I believe you…but…" her voice trailed off, maybe wondering if she should really say what she felt and risk hurting the man she loved.

"But," the husband said, (once again begging for an upper cut for the KO!)

She cleared her throat. I knew she was trying so hard not to say what she wanted to say in a hurtful way.

"Well, if you love me so much. Could you maybe just wash the dishes every once in a while?"

She had said it, but it was kind of like taking her finger out of the dike…because what was in her heart came pouring out…

"Would YOU, every once in a while…" I heard her try to choke back a sob, "just do some laundry like you did when we were first married?" There was no stopping it now…

"Would it be possible, just every once in a while…not always but maybe once a month, just take the kids so I could have just an hour or two by myself?" she cried now.

Revealing the heart does that…it brings cleansing and she was doing a very good job trying to respect her husband but speak her mind at the same time. I was proud of her. I got teary eyed too which, is no surprise, since I tear up at the home reveals on HGTV.

Her husband WISELY let her cry and didn't SAY A WORD!!! (Good job buddy!) I was cheering for him…it's hard to hear truth, hard to hear where you've fallen short. This guy was no chicken and was wise enough to let her finish without interruption. We need more men like him; I think.

"I want to know," his wife continued, "that your words MEAN something, and…I know they do; I mean, I KNOW you love me but…" her head was down in her hands and she was outright crying. She looked up and said, "If you love me so much, could you just wash the dishes?"

This may seem like a real invasion of privacy to you. I was the proverbial "fly on the wall" and not necessarily in a room I wanted to be in. Now, I've been discipled my friends, and I know when I should not remain in a room when two people have an issue to work out. But in this case, I had to hear what the resolution would be…I can't tell you why…it's like I was supposed to be here.

She fished into her purse for a tissue and looked frustrated. Her husband was ready however and

"Ahhh, the knight in shining armor!" handed her a handkerchief…a HANDKERCHIEF!!! And, it was clean too! She looked at him and smiled and wiped her eyes and nose. That's when I peeked a little lower (that dadgum menu was in my way!) and saw tears in his eyes.

He reached over to his wife and held her hand. He didn't speak, although she looked at him as he looked down at their hands and fingers intertwined.

"I'm such a bumbler!" he said to her raising his eyes. "Yes, of course…of COURSE I will do all of that and more!" he pulled her into his arms. "Sweetheart, can you ever forgive me? I've been too busy…just too busy!"

They hugged and she sighed a sigh of relief. She had been heard, and in humility he had seen his error.

Listen to me, any person younger than 95 reading this…

You need to understand your significant other's Love Language! To this woman, her love language was "Acts of Service". She didn't need to HEAR he loved her, she needed to SEE he loved her by doing things for her.

A summary of the Five Love Languages from "gotquestions.org" gives a pretty good summary.

I encourage you to purchase the book by Gary Chapman, *The Five Love Languages*.

https://www.christianbook.com/languages-secret-that-lasts-new-edition/gary-chapman

To end my story with a happy ending, the husband said he was going to put on his calendar every week to take the children and let his wife make plans.

She told him, "Oh, I don't need THAT much time alone…I want to spend it with YOU!"

A big smile broke out on her face… "Maybe just a few hours a month to myself!" He promised and I saw him take out his phone, in front of her and put in a reminder.

She began to laugh, and at that moment, she gave him HIS love language, "I just knew you would hear me out…YOU ARE THE MOST WONDERFUL MAN…GOD HAS BLESSED ME SO MUCH WITH YOU!"

(Words of Affirmation), now he wept as she held his head in her hands.

"I always want to take care of you sweetheart" he said, sobbing in her arms. His actions healed her heart, her words healed his soul and I have no doubt that other activities took their course later that day that I would have no business being privy to.

Talk to your spouse… Listen to each other. Learn their love language! You know, I ruined one marriage not doing it…I will never make that mistake again.

How about you?

Hidden Treasures

I drove this morning to an apartment complex where I was going to be de-odorizing a vacant apartment before some new tenants rented it. When I drove up, I did all of the usual things I do. I made an inventory of all my equipment, checked my extension cords to be sure there were no frays or lose wires.

I made sure I had my gas mask, because the fumes; even though all natural, can damage your lungs. I also checked and calibrated my air/gas detector to make sure it was charged up.

The air/gas detector is a pretty important piece of equipment. In the business I'm in, the air is measured by "parts per million". My equipment releases negatively charged ions into the air, unites with the hydrogen peroxide and creates a powerful agent that literally "scrubs" every surface. It is so strong it can pass through drywall, through carpet and into attic spaces.

For this reason, I wear a full NIOSH face mask with a breather unit on it to protect my eyes, face and lungs.

I sound like Darth Vader when I wear it. "Luke…I'm your FATHER", (Yes, I say it every time I put it on…)

I entered the apartment and began setting up the equipment, trying to be efficient with my time and making sure that AC filters were removed and installing vaporizers to spray hydrogen peroxide into the air to be circulated throughout the two-bedroom apartment.

When I opened the door where the furnace unit and water heater were located, I saw the cold air return directly beneath the door and headed back out to my truck to get my nut drivers and remove the cover and take out the air filter.

Can't leave an old air filter in a unit, or it just defeats the purpose of de-odorizing.

As I walked out to get my toolbox, I had a kind of sad feeling and I couldn't begin to tell you why at the time. But the closer I got to my truck, the sadder I became. This had been a good morning so far.

It was Friday for crying out loud…who wouldn't be happy today…right? I stopped and shot off one of my bullet prayers.

"Lord, whatever this is, if I'm worrying about my son Josiah (he's a police officer), or whatever…please just give me a peace and let joy return."

That was it, no angels appeared singing…just, my toolbox and a sip of my water.

As I entered the apartment again, the heaviness came over me so much that I sat down on the floor in the living room and leaned against the wall.

"Lord, I feel so sad…so heavy, what is this?" I asked. No answer…no inkling of what was happening.

I sighed heavily and started playing worship music on my phone… (right after Rocky Mountain High by John Denver…had to finish that song!) I stood and walked over to the cold air intake and began removing the cover to remove the filter.

As the last nut came off I lifted off the cover and it revealed an absolutely filthy filter, filled with dust and wrappers and hair and …yuck! I put work gloves on before I touched that nasty thing, but I noticed a folded half sheet of paper pressed against the dirty filter and I pulled it off and crumpled it in my hand as I removed the filter and took it outside. The heavy feeling had lifted all was well again.

I put it all down and finished my set up, being sure to set the temperature for 78 degrees and unplugging the smoke detector. All the machines were humming and I put on my mask, checked the air quality in the room started the vaporizers and pulled the apartment door closed and locked it. I would have to return tonight around 10pm to reset my machines since they only have a ten-hour timer.

I had locked the door and forgotten to return the key to the maintenance office. I got a call on my cell from the manager explaining that the property had an electronic key monitor and it had gone off telling him a key had left the premises. I apologized and ran it back over from another client's car lot where I was working.

When I returned the key, I had hastily picked up the sheet of paper I had removed from the filter along with the keys and happened to glance at it quickly before I threw it away.

There handwritten was a short note, 5/12/15:

"Sorry I couldn't run with you today, but my headaches were pretty bad. They seem to be taking me away from my favorite times with you AND your mother. I'll get back out there in a few days. Love being your running buddy!" Dad.

I told the guy, I had found an old, expired debit card a back-scrub brush and this note. The maintenance manager took the card and threw it and the brush away and was about to toss the note when he read it.

He said, "Hey, these people moved to 03-1331…would you just see if they want these? You pass right by it as you leave the property?"

I'm sorry, but my initial thought was he just wanted me to do his job and was being lazy. I said yes but wasn't enthusiastic about it. He handed me back the expired card, the brush and the note and I searched for the apartment and saw a lady just enter it and shut the door as I was driving up.

I walked up to the door and here came that feeling again... sadness. I knocked and a woman in her late thirties or very early forties answered. I smiled. I told her my name and what I did for the apartment complex and that I had evidently been preparing her old apartment for rental again when I ran across these three items.

"The maintenance manager thought you might like to have these."

She looked at the card and chuckled and said, "thank goodness that's expired!" and then bent it up and threw it away and told me to toss the brush in the dumpster.

I said, "I thought that's what you'd say, just didn't want to do it without asking, some people lose valuable things sometimes and want them back!"

I thanked her and turned to go as she looked quickly at the note. I was at the end of the sidewalk when I heard her say, "Sir? Could you come back for a moment?"

I walked back, thinking maybe I'd dropped something. She looked at me and asked, "Where did you find this?"

I explained the cold air return and how it looked like it had been sucked into it and had been there a while. She was quiet and placed her hand over her mouth while reading the note over and over to herself. I could tell it was an emotional thing for her…that note. I didn't want to break the silence and so I just stood there.

In my head I heard the Lord say, "Just wait." So, I did.

She looked up at me after she had composed herself and said, "My husband, passed away three years ago. He and my son did EVERYTHING together, they played tennis, and swam and ran together. My husband died of a brain hemorrhage in his sleep the very next day 5/13/15." She was strong because she did not tear up. She was very deliberate with her words and spoke slowly. "My son graduated and is at Auburn now as a freshman this year…he is a walk on member of the track team."

She smiled ear to ear. I smiled too and told her how proud her husband would have been. "Oh Yes!" She beamed, "Jim was at every single game or meet for our son Drew, they were sports nuts…both of them!"

Her eyes narrowed when she spoke next.

"I'm going to frame this and give it to my son…it's kind of like his dad sent a letter from heaven!"

I said, "Only he doesn't have a headache now!"

She laughed and said, 'You're right…he doesn't!" She shook my hand and said, "You've given the world to me today…thank you!"

I told her about the feeling right before I found it. She shook her head and became serious after I said this.

She bowed her head, took my hands in hers and said, "Thank you father, for giving this man hearing ears…and thank you for your Son Jesus!"

Well, I am NOT a strong woman…so of course tears flowed down my face…I'm such a baby!

I walked away, after I had thanked her for her wonderful prayer. She asked if I was a Christian and I told her yes.

She kind of shouted as I walked away, "There are lots of us Doug, and there are more coming! God is going to fill this earth with us Doug!"

I turned to her and shouted, "Like the water covers the seas!"

She shouted "Hallelujah!" lifting her hands to the sky.

All I could say was, "Hallelujah!" …and walking away, of course, I cried again…baby!

What if No One Knows Your Name?

I was discussing with some friends the other evening at dinner about the proofreading of my children's book. I have been talking about releasing it for over two years, but it has been important to me to make sure it reads with the intention I wish for it to read, and that it can be understood by children. Children are the true field of harvest…we can impress their hearts with truth and nothing will steal it from them, even decades after they have been touched by it. If you wish to change the world, reach children with the seeds of Gospel truth…any way you can!

They had kind comments for me… my dinner friends that is and my heart was warmed by their encouragement. But around 3 in the morning I was awakened by…what I can only explain as the voice of the Lord.

He asked, "What if no one knows your name?"

It was as though someone had shaken me to consciousness.

Blinking awake, He repeated the question, although it was unnecessary, because God is confident that when He speaks, we fully understand what has been said.

"What if no one knows your name?"

The question broke me…it reduced me to tears and I convulsed as God revealed my heart to me. It wasn't just a question; it was the Holy Spirit tearing open the veil of my soul to reveal to me what lay beneath the public persona of "humility" I had portrayed for too long.

God is the only One I know of Who; can tear asunder seemingly innocent motives, to show their maggot filled interiors. My interior was exposed in all of its nakedness and I caught a glimpse of what it will be like standing before the Judgment Seat of Christ…exposed.

Like always, the Lord was gentle after wielding His sword. Quivering raw flesh was healed over and calm wrapped around me like a warm blanket. I was exhausted and yet, I received the energy (this is the only way to explain it), to sit up in bed as He asked me, "What if I am the only one to know what you have written?"

"What if your books aren't celebrated?"

"Will you be disappointed leaving your legacy in My hands after you die?"

These questions were all about my motives. Why do I write…and turning this to you my dear reader, what will happen if no one knows YOUR name after you are gone?

You and I are no better than those who have gone before us…are we? Some of the greatest people who have ever lived were only known after they died. I give you some examples to ponder God's searching question…

"What if no one knows YOUR name?"

°Although the publication of his one book brought this American author, poet and philosopher modest success, his political writings had little impact during his lifetime. He earned his living by WORKING IN A PENCIL FACTORY, lecturing occasionally and by publishing essays in newspapers and journals. He never made much money, which probably suited him fine. But nearly three decades after his death, Henry Stephens Salt wrote a biography of this man, earning him great posthumous fame.

His political writings went on to influence leaders like Mohandas Gandhi, John F. Kennedy, Martin Luther King Jr., U.S. Supreme Court Justice William O. Douglas, and Leo Tolstoy, as well as artists and authors including Edward Abbey, Willa Cather, Marcel Proust, William Butler Yeats, Sinclair Lewis, Ernest Hemingway, Upton Sinclair, E.B. White, Lewis Mumford, Frank Lloyd Wright, Alexander Posey and Gustav Stickley.

Not to mention all of us who love to take a meandering meditative walk in the woods.[ii] The man's name; Henry David Thoreau, and like many who reason deep into the night with only themselves to critique their work, his influence spoke loudly to future generations, proving it appears, that the gifts that God gives cannot be silenced.

°It would be misleading to say that the German born composer died before he was famous, since he was acclaimed for his talent as an organist. But he was not known as a composer, yet that is what he is most famous for now. Few of his works were published during his lifetime.

It wasn't until 1829 when German composer Felix Mendelssohn reintroduced this, composers "Passion According to St. Matthew" that he began to receive posthumous praise for the work of his musical compositions. Now he is generally regarded as one of the major composers of the Baroque period, if not one of the greatest composers of all time.[iii] His name was Johann Sebastian Bach.

It was left for others to discover his true genius, and he was never recognized for the very area he loved the most…composing music for God during his lifetime. But one sitting upon the Throne in Glory knew his name, and there is no doubt that a portion of the music of heaven will have been written by him when we arrive there after our deaths.

°Although the American-born writer from New York City had a flirtation with early success, his writing career took a nosedive after the publication of his second book. He continued writing, but after the age of 35, critical and financial success from writing remained elusive. By 1876, all of his books were out of print. All told, he earned a mere $10,000 from writing.

He eventually took a job as a customs inspector on the New York docks, which finally brought him a secure income. He held the position for 19 years.

In the 1920s, a biography written by Raymond Weaver about him brought renewed attention to the writer and sparked the revival by which the man finally got his due. His opus, "Moby-Dick," is now hailed as one of the world's literary masterpieces.[iv]

His name; Herman Melville. A writer of adventure whose greatest work awaited his death before it would make him famous.

°The Austrian-born lover of God, discovered the basic principles of heredity through experiments in his monastery garden, but both his Law of Segregation (dominant and recessive traits are passed on randomly from parents to offspring) and the Law of Independent Assortment (traits are passed on independently of other traits) were little promoted and mostly misunderstood by the contemporary scientific community.

In 1868, he became a school abbot and between his schoolwork and failing eyesight, he pretty much abandoned science. Upon his death, his work was largely unknown. Yet during the ensuing years, other scientists began to refer to his early work; his system eventually proved to be one of the foundational principles of biology, and many consider him to be the father of modern genetics.[v]

His name; Gregor Johann Mendel. Every student of science now reveres his name, but during his time on earth, he was ignored…even laughed at by the scientific community, but God had other plans.

°She is one of America's national treasures, the poet had a mere 10 poems published while alive, and she may have been unaware of their publication. While she was extremely prolific as a poet and regularly shared her work with friends and family, she was not publicly recognized during her lifetime.

By the middle of her life, she lived in almost total physical isolation from the outside world, but no one is sure why she chose such a reclusive life. Upon her death, her sister Lavina discovered 40 hand-bound volumes of nearly 1,800 of her poems; although Lavinia had promised to burn all of her correspondence, fortunately for poetry lovers everywhere, no such instructions were given for her poems.

Her name was Emily Dickenson. You know her, but her contemporaries did not.

The first volume of her work was published posthumously in 1890 and the last in 1955; she remains one of the most highly regarded of American poets. [vi]

°Born in New York City and raised in France, she moved to Chicago in 1956 where she spent most of her life as a nanny. But when not tending to her charges, the unassuming caretaker took to the streets, cataloging the people and sites with her handy Rolleiflex camera.

Eventually, she became somewhat destitute, but was ultimately taken care of by three of the children she had cared for earlier in her life. No one who knew her was aware of her secret life as a street photographer, a documentary-type genre of photography that relies on candid shots of strangers in public.

Taking snapshots well into the late 1990s. She would leave behind more than 100,000 negatives, in addition to other forms of media.

In 2007, a young man working on a historical book of Chicago bought a mystery box of 30,000 of her prints and negatives from a thrift auction house that had acquired the media from a storage facility, where she had been delinquent with her fees.

Following her death, the man figured out who she was through an obituary, and he began sharing her work. Since then, her photographs have been exhibited all over the world, have appeared in print in numerous countries, and there is now a book and movie about her and her work.[vii]

Her name's Vivian Maier. The fact that you have to search for who she is in a search engine, tells you that greatness is not always rewarded with fame.

°He became embroiled in a dispute with his creditor, and the man sued and won control of his workshop and half the books printed. Thus, he was bankrupted and lived out the rest of his years in obscurity. He died poor in 1468 and was buried in a church cemetery which was later destroyed and the grave lost.[viii]

His name on earth, Johann Gutenberg…inventor of the printing press. Unknown to any in his generation but applauded by myriads of angels and His Lord upon his entrance to glory. The world had been turned upside down by this servant who took the Scriptures; denied to the common man by a cruel religious system and placed them within reach for others to hold in their own hands.

His printing press had turned on the light and ushered in the Renaissance, the "Re-birth" of Christian thought in the world. But today, we cannot even find where he is buried.

°Finally, there was 1920's bluesman Blind Willie Johnson. His desire was to become a famous musician, even though his stepmother had blinded him when he was seven years old by throwing lye in his eyes after his father had beaten her for being with another man.

He died penniless, of pneumonia after sleeping bundled in wet newspapers in the ruins of his house that had burned down. He died never knowing NASA in 1978 decided to include on the Golden Record carrying "sounds of the Planet Earth" on Voyager, Johnson's song, "Dark Was The Night, Cold Was The Ground" along with an array of music including Gregorian chants and Chuck Berry.[ix]

He was no one of note during his pain filled life, but his music left our solar system just 10 years ago. Such is the faithfulness of a God of Mercy and Justice.

****

After my literal "awakening" early this morning, what I realize now is that God is not only the giver of ideas, inventions, music, art, books and breakthroughs, He will also not share His glory with another. He is the light giver, the one who saves the world. Our part in these endeavors is given by God as those privileged to <u>share in His work</u>, but NOT in His glory. I recognize that I write for an audience of One, and while we hope for recognition; regardless of the areas of our endeavors, it is God who will decide if our names will be known anywhere but in eternity.

If you write, sing, dance, paint, create or labor with intensity for seemingly no public acclaim, please know that who you are and what you do is NOT insignificant to God. He is the one who raises up the lowly, and to those obscured by injustice, He will sweep it away and show your work proudly to an eternity of the saints.

If you labor in prayer in secret bringing about spiritual revolution, if you preach in a small church, with a tiny congregation that we will never read about, or if you quietly labor as a missionary to peoples great or small, YOUR reward is great in the Kingdom of God.

It does not matter how many books you sell, how many songs become hit records, how many paintings seem to be stuffed into your closet gathering dust.

There is a "God Who Sees" Who is well able to make our meager offerings into masterpieces to feed the imaginations of the masses. He will make your work worthwhile…if you are brave enough not to care too much, whether or not you are famous in this world.

The Purpose of Money

Many years ago, when I was a young man and my wife and I were missionaries to Brazil, I am sorry to say that I lived by faith far more than I do today. We had raised support; going from church to church to tell them of our vision for reaching young college students on the Universities of Rio and Sao Paulo.

God had been very faithful to us and every month, our needs were met and we were able to give away some of it to help others.

However, it was no cake walk.

Living on a fixed income always presented a challenge and of course, we just couldn't spend any way we wanted to. While all of the necessities were covered by our monthly support, some of the things we would have liked to have gotten just had to wait because they weren't priorities. New clothing or shoes for example, were way down on the list of priorities, so we just put those things out of our mind and decided to be content with what we had.

Occasionally, one of the overseers of our ministry would fly down to check on us and literally, to just love on a young 20 something couple who had left everything behind to follow where Jesus led. On one such occasion, a dear, gentle and loving man named Joe Smith, flew down to visit our team in Rio.

Joe and Katie Smith were; in my 20 something opinion, the surrogate "Dad and Mom" of our ministries. Senior to my wife and I by 30 years, Joe and Katie would come in with smiles on their faces and never failed to bring much needed encouragement to this young inexperienced writer.

There was always a hug from sweet Katie, whose eyes always glistened when she would see us and a light kiss on the cheek from a woman whose true ministry was to take the love of Angels wherever she went. I cannot help but have tears of sweetness from her memory.

Joe, a former chemist/engineer at GAF, was kind…his smiles were genuine, but he had no room for self-pity…not for himself and not in us. His firm handshake and hug were authentic, and while his discernment was keen and could cut to the heart of a matter within a second, his desire to bless was second to none. I recall one particular trip that Joe and Katie made to our home in Sao Paulo.

Joe liked to run…in fact, at 50+ years of age, Joe demonstrated on several occasions. He and I would run through the University of Sao Paulo, across the statuary meadow and into the woods. Joe wouldn't just run…he would pointedly show you by running up foothills and over rocks, and around trees that you would be hard pressed to beat him.

I remember seeing Joe sitting at the front gate of our home in Sao Paulo, smiling ear to ear grin watching me slowly catch up to him. He had been sitting for 20 minutes I'm sure.

I tell you this about Joe and Katie because while I remember the kindness of them, there was one particular day on their visit that I remember most of all. It was the second to the last day they were in town.

We all went to the Shopping Mall Ibirapuera, and were walking around when Joe announced, "Okay, everyone gets tennis shoes today!"

We walked into a sports footwear store and he told us to pick out a pair of shoes. This was a huge deal to my wife and I. We hadn't had the money to buy anything new for over year. Joe and Katie laughed, and were having such fun. We then went to a nearby restaurant in the mall and sat to ate.

Joe was a final statement kind of teacher. He would always say things you would never forget like, "Why is it we always have time to do things over, but we don't have the time to do them right in the first place?" or, "We always judge others by their actions, but we judge ourselves by the intention of our hearts."

See what I mean…you don't forget those things, they are from the Throne of God, spoken directly to your heart.

On this occasion, Joe looked at this fledgling couple, probably doubtful that our work would ever make a difference in the world and smiled, saying, "You know what money is good for?" My wife and I looked at each other and before we could answer. "For making memories. Money is for loving people and making memories."

He said, "I know you two, look at us. 'Wow, what would it be like to be able to bless people and give away from ourselves…well, you will.' You will, someday, find people along your path that are doing the best they can, and God is going to give you the money to bless them and make a memory."

The next day, as they were leaving, Katie of course gave us hugs and kisses and she looked at me like a mom would look at a son smiled and said, "You're doin' good Doug, we're proud of you."

Joe would look sternly, with no time for hugs or tears and said, "Carry On!" turned quickly on his heel and walked away.

I was in my room in the hotel the other day, when a knock from housekeeping interrupted my concentration on something I was doing on my computer. I opened the door, and quickly said hello and went back to my computer.

She began arranging the room, making the bed, cleaning the bathroom and I heard in my head my old friend Joe Smith say, "Money is for loving people and making memories".

When I turned to look at the housekeeper, she was almost finished and I looked at her and said, "Samantha, (she had a nametag on folks…I'm not THAT tuned in…YET!), I continued, "you and your husband have been very concerned about finances lately…but I want you to know, that God knows the needs of your home and your child and He cares so much, that He wants to make a memory with you today."

With that, I pulled out all the money in my pocket and pressed it into her hand and said, "I was not even supposed to be in the room right now Samantha…for some reason I came up an hour early to work on my computer, and you showed up."

She broke down into tears and was sobbing so hard she couldn't speak.

I gave her a hug and said, "Sweetie, every young couple has difficult times…but Jesus…he just KNOWS what we need and when we need it."

She looked up with tear-stained eyes and told me her husband was training in the Army and they had one child and… I can hardly say what I am going to say right now as I write because I am so overcome with emotion., "We don't have the money right now but I wanted to get my little boy some.... Tennis shoes."

****

I'm not as kind as Katie, and nowhere as good of a mentor as Joe…but as she broke down again telling me how she could catch up bills now and was glorifying God saying, "I had just prayed this morning…" and that is all she could say.

I gave her one more *Katie* hug and told her. "Samantha, money is for loving people and making memories… someday, you'll do this same thing for others."

As the door closed, I am absolutely sure that I felt a hand on my back as I stood weeping in my hotel room and heard a soft but firm voice say…

… "Carry On".

When God Interrupts Our Plans...

Back in the day, I was on my way to church when I had to stop off at Kroger to pick something. As I entered, I saw the cashier was trying to scan a greeting card for a woman.

I quickly re-focused and walked to the aisle, got my stuff and headed for the check out. (This was before the self, check-out aisle). There was the same cashier trying to scan the same card...sliding it over and over and over again over the scanner and getting nowhere.

I turned to look at the woman who was miraculously standing there waiting. She looked haggard, her eyes were red, she had on house slippers, she obviously had come early so she could get in and get out quickly.

The card she was trying to buy was a "sympathy" card. Someone had died... she was distressed and I simply said to her, "I'm so sorry for your loss."

She turned to me. "My nephew drowned over the weekend, in the family pool. My sister is devastated... and, I can't be there for her." Tears filled her eyes as she spoke. "Our jobs won't allow for us to travel at this time, and all I can do is send this card, until I can go next week." Her voice trailed off.

The cashier had gone to get another identical card, and tried to scan it with no success. I asked the woman, "May I pray for you?" She nodded.

I prayed. "God of Peace fill her heart and the family's." It wasn't an eloquent prayer; in fact, it was quite clumsy. I saw that three or four other people who were behind me, had bowed their heads, along with the cashier, and as soon, as I finished, I said "Amen," the card scanner beeped and registered!

The people behind me, along with the cashier, said "AMEN!" And, off she went into the early morning, and I never saw her again. but here is my point...

****

Many of the supernatural things that happened in the Bible, took place "while He was walking" or "as He entered the city". In other words, most of the miracles that Jesus did; took place while they were on their way to another town, or just "doing life".

Everyday life is where things happen. Baristas making coffee, cashiers are cashiering, bankers are banking, donut dunkers are dunking. Life is busy, it has activity it has action...no time to stop by the side of the road for a sermon, or a quick word of wisdom...no time for anything except "get 'er done!"

That's why Christianity is such an action packed, full contact sport. Life happens in milliseconds..."pumping gas and on your way" kind of action. Over the years, I realize that God has "set me up" a hundred million times to show love, to show His power, and I; like the bright light bulb that I am, MISSED everyone, of them.

Somewhere along the way, the light came on however...and I realized that I have to take advantage of the 5 seconds at the register while waiting in line, or the 3 minutes at the gas pump or at Starbucks...or wherever to show God's love and power. It's telling the girl at 5 Guys last night I appreciated how she was always smiling...I got her laughing and at that moment the idea that we were complete strangers melted away, and for a moment we were just two fellow sojourners on the same road who took time to laugh.

The fruit of the Spirit is love, joy, peace, patience, kindness, goodness, faithfulness, gentleness and self-control. Kindness opens so many doors for God to show His power; it ain't even funny! All it takes...literally, is two open eyes and the willingness to talk first. It doesn't even take particular courage...just open your mouth and watch God fill it!

Curiosity Works in Our Favor

I've attended a lot of different church services in my lifetime and the spectrum of believers goes from Traditional to Pentecostal… from Catholic to Presbyterian. From common everyday sensible including the Doxology all the way to wacky, screaming and pew jumpin'; smack yo mamma wif a Bible in da head Holy rollers.

In most cases and across the entire universe of Christian denominational spaghetti-intertwined doctrinal statements of faith… (say that five times quickly), I find only a few things really important for me to stand firmly behind. Of course; the Lordship of Jesus stands above all as well and the Lordship of His Word.

Which brings me to a conversation I had today with a guy named Earl, (He goes by the name "Shark" because of the gorgeous tattoo of a shark on his right arm and, in his own words, "my male parental unit must have been "effing crazy" to have named me after himself!") Shark was with his wife Tondra and their child…Rocket.

Shark and I began our conversation over a graphic novel he was reading and that had caught my eye while walking by his table at Barnes and Noble. The graphic novel was, the very FIRST of books to be called graphic novels from all the way back to 1978 called, "A Contract with God" by author Will Eisner.

Shark had purchased the book from a used book dealer in Nashville and was carefully leafing through it while his wife and child ate chocolate chip cookies and Tondra sipped a cappuccino.

Being intentionally nosy, I asked what a book entitled "A Contract with God" was about. Shark explained it was an anthology of four, non-related stories about Jewish inhabitants of a tenement building which were largely made up of Eisner's memories growing up.

It seemed to be a very melancholy book and Shark sipped his demi tasse with an air of discernment as he looked at me curiously. "What makes an obviously Protestant looking gentleman like yourself take interest in a graphic novel sitting furtively on my table?" adding to his comment quickly, "No offense intended."

I was so completely impressed by both his demeanor, his honesty AND his use of the word "furtively" while referring to a book, that, I smiled and answered I would tell him if he would let me buy him another espresso. Shark nodded appreciatively.

I returned to the table to find Tondra and Rocket sitting at the two-seat table. Rocket sat on Tondra's lap. Shark reached out to take his coffee and asked me to pull up a seat. I introduced myself and explained what "BioSweep" meant monogrammed on my shirt.

Shark pulled at his goatee. "Okay, so, why the question, why the coffee and why the interest at all?" Again, impressed with his honesty.

I felt he deserved the absolute and complete truth to his question. So, I told him. "I wanted to know what the book was about, because I wanted to discuss views about God with you. That's it…no other reason."

His eyes narrowed somewhat and he pushed his weight back on the back legs of his chair. "Wow…you didn't try to even hide it!"

I laughed. "So, you already knew the answer to your own question?"

Shark looked at Tondra. "Tondy…an honest Christian!" smiling and gesturing toward me with his head.

His wife looked at me. "Imagine that…"

I decided to not ask what he meant…because I already knew.

We live in a time when people are skeptical of anything that sounds like traditional Christianity, especially if that Christianity has to do with a salt box church, being preached at every Sunday and the lack of results in society.

Who can blame them? I don't.

Millennials comment they have seen too much hypocrisy and want something "authentic", which means; I suppose, a search for a genuine lifestyle that lives what it purports to believe. Again, I can't say I disagree with them.

For too long, it has been my observation that Christianity is a "graying" religion without adventure. There seems to be a lot of activity and bigger and bigger "Mega" churches, with lots of programs and large attendance numbers.

But when one gets right down to it, who wants to belong to an organization? Is that what happened in Acts chapter 2 when the Holy Spirit fell upon the disciples in the upper room?

Did the Holy Spirit create an 501c3 that held itself aloof from society, spent most of its money on itself and its buildings and whose understanding of friendship centered on trying to get your acquaintances to a point where they would convert to your flavor of Christianity and start doing the same thing?

Did Jesus intend the Christian to relate mostly to those within the Church's walls and look with judgment upon those on the outside? If you ask modern outsiders today, they say a unanimous "yes." The "Church" in their opinion, appears to be unwilling to develop friendships with non-Christians.

There appears to be a "self-centeredness" that is not really interested in others except how they can get them into the church. They feel the church does not reach our culture because the church isn't a part of our culture, it is "apart' FROM our culture. There are wonderful exceptions to this rule, like Crossroads Church in Cincinnati, Ohio and others starting to pop up across our country.

In an online blog called, Thom S. Rainer, "Growing Healthy Churches Together." (thomrainer.com) he has nailed the problem exactly in his blog, "What Do Non-Christians Really Think About Us?"

(https://thomrainer.com/2013/06/what-do-non-christians-really-think-of-us/).

He writes: I consider myself a very blessed man in a number of ways. This blog has become one of my great blessings. One of the reasons I love this blog community is the variety of people who interact on it. There has been an increase in the number of people who aren't Christians who comment on various posts.

I want to share with you the perspective of one young woman on how she views Christians. These comments come directly from her comments on some of my posts. They have not been changed.

***Unfortunately, I can't add a comment here, so I'm posting it here. These articles and this part, is a bit far from what the book is about. I like the book, but this actual chapter, if we can call it that, is not relevant to the entire book. It takes the reader away from the true meaning of the book. (JUST A HEADS UP)

On Being Selfish, Not Really Interested in Others

I remember a rather outspoken evangelical Christian young woman I worked with – I'd just moved to town, and we went to a movie together. Each week she invited me to her church, and I didn't want to offend her by saying "No thanks." As it was, I had Buddhist activities one Sunday and I was mentoring a young girl two other Sundays, but that theoretically left a Sunday open. We only worked together for 3 months, and it never worked out. I went to a different job.

She showed up there one night, and jumped right to the church invite. No "Hey, how've you been? Haven't seen you in a while!" Nope – just "Do you want to come to church with me this weekend?" Since I was on to her game, I decided to play. I said, "Sure, I'll go to church with you, because I'm interested in seeing what you're interested in. That's what friends do, after all. And I'm sure you'll want to come with me to a Buddhist meeting to see what I'm interested in, right?"

"Oh no!" she replied. "I just love the Lord so much!"

"Well," I said, "then there's no point in me going to your church because I'm not interested in either becoming a Christian or joining your church." I never saw her again.

That's how far Christian friendship extends – I've seen it over and over and over. Christians look at everyone else as if they've got targets painted on their foreheads. Nobody likes being hunted down or treated like someone else's project. We don't need to drop all our beliefs just to accept yours, and we don't need to become more like you just to be acceptable people, worthy of being regarded as people instead of targets. Love does not seek to create clones of itself. Selfishness does.

On Being Self-Centered and Judgmental

Keep your religious beliefs to yourself. If I have any interest in what you believe, I'll ask you. And if I don't ask you, then go right ahead and assume that your "witnessing" will be unwelcome. I'm sure that you like whatever you believe very much, and I'm very happy that you like it. However, just as your favorite flavor of ice cream is not necessarily going to be mine, I wish you would assume that I'm just as content with my own beliefs (or lack thereof) as you are with yours. Why not ask me first what *I* believe? Why not show an interest in what's interesting to me instead of expecting me to always be interested in what YOU'RE interested in? Christians are so selfish and self-centered! Tell me – when was the last time an atheist rang your doorbell to tell you about his worldview? The reason the world hates Christians is because they behave badly, they're rude, boorish, arrogant, conceited, full of themselves, ignorant, and judgmental. Go ahead – accuse me of being judgmental now. Doesn't matter – I don't claim to follow a belief system that has actual rules AGAINST being judgmental, so it's *fine* for me to be!

On Being Unwilling to Develop True Friendships with Non-Christians

As a mother of young children in a homeschooling environment, we found ourselves surrounded by Christians. Of course, the kids would become friends and we moms would chat while they played. Without a single exception, this "acquaintanceship" only progressed to the point that I had to make it clear that no, I would not "acceptjesusasmypersonalsavior" (quotation marks, mine) and no, I would not be attending their church. Then the Christians never called again, and I was left to explain to my sad children why their new friends wouldn't be playing with them anymore.

When my son was just 6, the boys down the street told him he was not allowed to play with them because he wasn't a Christian. I went down to see what was going on (because my 4-yr-old daughter was going to go down there and teach those boys a lesson!) and I confirmed that what my son had reported was indeed what they'd said. And the mother of one was right out in the front yard, 25 feet from me, pretending to be very focused on trimming some plants. She never said a word.

Finally, the 6-yr-old girl across the street told my kids, ages 7 and 9, that if they weren't Christians, they would be going to hell. She certainly learned the "Good News". And you Christians wonder why we non-Christians avoid you?? HINT: It's not because we're intimidated by your awesomeness and are just sitting here, pining for you, wishing you would like us. We already know you don't.[1]"

Stories like those sting...

I can tell you from personal experience that every story in that blog is true because I have personally seen countless examples from my own life where almost the same identical things happened…except I was the perpetrator! As I look back on what my idea of "witnessing" was, I recognize that instead of seeking out the lost and loving them unconditionally, I had been just another reason for a non-Christians to throw rocks at every church they passed by.

Well, I finally went through a time when, for numerous reasons, I took a break from church attendance. I had gone through a divorce, I had been told by many of my old friends in the church how "selfish and self-centered" I was for divorcing, and from having a friendship where we spent fun evenings watching movies with each other and sharing meals at each other's homes, I was shunned, and not only by them, but having felt it was their duty to inform the rest of the congregation; the rest of my old church friends rejected me as well.

I moved back to my old hometown and in a time of gut wrenching depression, I sought to rebuild my personal world. I began a business; a winery and renovated a 1930's gas station into a dining room. I stayed away from church in all honesty due to the sting of the relationships that ended when they considered my Christianity "tainted". I felt no desire to ever build that kind of shallow relationship again. There are many whom I still block on Facebook.

I met my wife, Mary Ann, and we began facing the world and connecting with new friends and started our lives together. Along the way, the people who I had previously sought to "win to Jesus" were the only people I had relationships with. I worked with them and laughed with them. I heard em cuss and they heard me cuss too. I discovered my "worldly" friends took a genuine interest in me. They were fellow travelers, and listening and being listened to were the dues we paid to become a part of the fraternity. And it WAS a fraternity!

I suppose if you want to know the truth, I shook off every vestige of Western Christianism, (notice I didn't say Christianity), in other words I shook off "Churchianity" along with all of its false friendship and self-righteous nose lifting and became an authentic person again. I stopped associating with those who, if I didn't quake and shake like they did, they questioned whether I had been filled the Holy Spirit. Someone who was not afraid to rub shoulders with sinners, because I finally had recognized I was a sinner too! And something wonderful began to happen…

I began to discover my personality coming alive without the pressure to "invite people to church" and without the need to always mention how "Jesus had changed my life". I began connecting individually with Jesus again and as I did that, I began to really connect with the people that I worked with and total strangers in the marketplace. I began to realize that I felt free, and I don't mean free to sin, but I knew that the perfectionism of being a" perfect Christian" had been a hoax. It was a lie of the devil to convince me I would get infected by the world if I let my guard down and became friends with people in the world who didn't attend church. The hoax was designed to keep me away from the very people Jesus wanted to reach…with love.

You and I are fallen creations. Even with the Blood of Jesus, we are going to sin and mess up and hit our fingers with hammers and cuss and the Lord loves us and asks us to surrender again…and we do. But holding ourselves up to the world as some nice smelling, clean fingernailed dandy doesn't do anything but tell them, "We don't want you or your kids to infect our children!". And when we do that, whether or not we realize we're doing it, people will stay away from us in crowds. Our "Fallenness" is about all we have in common with the world and while Jesus said "Love not the world, or the things of the world"… He was not talking about withholding love from the people IN the world.

If all you needed to do in order to fulfill the Great Commission was to love people, engage them in conversation, help them fill their gas tanks with gas, take the initiative and smile and see each one as a unique creation of God without inviting them to church or inquiring whether or not they were saved…COULD YOU BE ALRIGHT WITH THAT? Could their prolonged exposure to that type of Christian behavior bring them to the point where they might want to know about the God you serve? Could that be making disciples?

I am convinced Paul's message in I Corinthians 3:6 is 90 percent PLANTING and WATERING, *"What then is Apollos? And what is Paul? They are servants through whom you believed, as the Lord has assigned to each his role.* I planted the seed and Apollos watered it, but God made it grow. *So neither he who plants nor he who waters is anything, but only God, who makes things grow.....".* I think the reason the church has turned off the world in some part is because everybody want to be the reaper…everybody has a warped idea about what their "Christian Duty" is. I have seen God do some very incredible things as I have just loved people and enjoyed relationship with them. I have stopped trying to be responsible for everyone's salvation and I now leave that up to God.

I am titling my new book, "God Lives in the Unremarkable Moments" because all of us have prayed at one time or another "God, I want to do something great for you in this life". If you haven't prayed that, then you have prayed something close to it. The only problem with the prayer is, God doesn't need you to do some great big thing…He needs you to do the daily, relationship thing in unremarkable moments throughout your life with people you meet every day. God lives in the quiet, unseen, unremarkable moments of our lives…and it is precisely in those moments, where; if you are in relationship with Jesus, God will use you and your humanity to touch people in supernatural ways. It has been a real joy to see people open up like flowers since I began this experiment, and God amazes me every day with opportunities to show He cares about people. I ask you to read about some of those opportunities in my upcoming book.

By the way, I am back at church, and loving the freedom of worshiping Jesus because of who He is and my new understanding of what: in my opinion the Church was designed to be. As John Jefferson Davis in his book, "Christ's Victorious Kingdom" states:

"...any amelioration of social evils is not the result of immanent forces at work within history, nor primarily merely human effort, but essentially is the result of the supernatural influence of the ascended Christ through His Word and Spirit, working *through His people*. A spiritually revitalized church is understood to have an increasingly positive impact on the surrounding world and it's structures through its PREACHING, SOCIAL MINISTRY AND THE EXAMPLE OF ITS OWN INNER LIFE." [1]

I spoke for another 20 minutes to Shark and Tondra…without attempting to invite them to a church or trying to lead them in "the sinner's prayer." Before I left, I DID do something unashamedly Christian. I walked to the Christian inspiration section and pulled down a book about a Jewish holocaust survivor who became a Christian and consequently changed millions of lives with her story. Her name was Corrie Ten Boom and the book was, "The Hiding Place.

I dropped it on Shark's table and asked him if he was an honest man. He shook my hand and said, "You won't find a more honest man!" I asked him if he had ever heard of Corrie Ten Boom. He said no. I asked him, instead of buying me an espresso, if he would buy the book and read it. He walked up to the cashier and paid for it immediately.

On my way out, he shoulder bumped me…said I was "white cake personified" at which I laughed until tears came to my eyes. I told him his picture was by the word "Bohemian" in the dictionary and he smiled really big and said, "Mazel tov!" I invited he and Tondra to dinner and we waved goodbye. Peace my Jewish brother…May the God of Abraham, Isaac and Jacob bring you to a true knowledge of the Living God Yeshua…and may you trust only in Him!

Alone in the Plaza...

When I was a young man, my wife and I traveled to Brazil and were missionaries with a campus ministry for 5 years. We raised support and we went in faith, believing that God would meet all our needs.

This was in July of 1980.

For two years we worked with another wonderful couple and others from the States to build a church and raise up leaders. It was a wonderful time but it required a LOT of faith to believe that God would take care of our every need. In the first place, I spoke Spanish, but in Brazil they speak Portuguese.

We took lessons but, we learned to speak the language by wading into the deep water of day to day activities and learning as we went about business. God always showed up, and even though my Brazilian friends would encouragement me that my Portuguese was improving, I was never quite sure that what I intended to say from the pulpit was exactly what was said!!! I laugh about it today that it was truly a miracle people came to Jesus through my Portuguese.

In 1982, we decided to outreach the city of Sao Paulo. Sao Paulo is the largest city in South America and today, boasts a population of over 12.18 million people. Realizing I couldn't afford a plane ticket to fly, I took a bus which was called a "Leito" which meant it had attendants like an airplane and was a "sleeper" bus. It was very nice and I settled into my seat for the roughly 9 hour trip.

In those days we had friends with a group called "Youth With A Mission" (YWAM) and I was told that when I arrived in Sao Paulo, a young man named; to the best of my recollection, Aristarchus…(this was over 30+ years ago, but it was a really "different" biblical name like that.), would meet me in the plaza next to the bus station.

I had never been in that city, I had never met this Aristarchus, I wasn't traveling with much money, I had no phone number for this man and somehow, I was supposed to recognize him, and he would recognize me, and then I would go to his home to sleep for the night.

Seemed reasonable to me at 25 years of age.

When I arrived at the plaza, I got off the bus and saw the plaza across the street. I don't know what I had expected, but we arrived super early in the morning at 2:30 am. As I looked across the street from the bus station, I thought I would see a person or two, but instead it was PACKED with people! I thought if I waited by the bus terminal, the plaza would clear out, but instead, it got busier!!

I prayed and asked the Lord to watch over me and to keep me from harm. Brazil, at least in those days, was infamous for getting robbed, or stabbed and robbed or held at gunpoint while you were robbed.

Thieves would get on buses and wait until the bus was on a lone stretch of road, then they would take out their guns and walk the aisle of the bus point a gun at you and demand cash, rings, jewelry of all kinds and they would simply shoot you if you resisted.

In one instance, they even shot a baby for crying…really bad dudes.

Remembering all of this as I walked into that crowded plaza, I nonetheless had a real peace inside. I looked just like the corn-fed white boy I was…and everyone in that plaza knew I must be crazy to be walking with two suitcases into a plaza and sitting on the steps of the fountain, apparently waiting for Aristarchus to find me.

Herein is a lesson I learned. God; sometimes, will not allow us to recognize the danger of our situation until we are past it. I'm not saying He always does that…I'm not sure God "always" does anything, and of course there was the youthful virtue of being "clueless' but I have to say I did not fear anything at that moment. He cannot however cure STUPID…but He does deliver us sometimes from it.

In the minute or two that I was sitting there at that fountain, I was approached by a man who stood staring at me. I stood up and was taller than he was. He had an even shorter man standing next to him. I asked him in my Indiana Portuguese accent, "Hello, Are you Aristarchus?" He said nothing and nodded up and down to the affirmative.

You would think I would ask for identification and a secret handshake, but of course, being me…I just believed him! Aren't you glad that God intervenes in our lives?

Like I said, I never recognized the danger I was in at the moment, but I was blithely walking like a goober obediently behind some guy who hadn't said a word. (You wonder how on earth I have survived this long don't you?)

As I pulled my luggage behind a me, we were almost to the edge of the plaza and were getting ready to walk down a long alleyway, when suddenly, I heard a voice call out, "Douglas!"

I turned around and a really tall, sharp chinned Brazilian walked quickly up to me and asked, "Are you Douglas?"

I said, "Yes, I am, who are you?"

He smiled. "Douglas, allow me to introduce you to my friend, Aristarchus!"

I looked at the tall guy, then behind him I saw a young guy, about my age, standing next to him.

I said to the tall guy, "I thought this was…"

I turned to introduce him to my chaperones, but they had taken off running down the alley. Aristarchus smiled at me and said "Ladrões," the Portuguese word for "Thieves".

I stood there blinking and after hearing Aristarchus say a few things, like the name of my ministry partner in Rio and some mutual acquaintances, I realized he was the REAL Aristarchus.

I was reprimanded gently by my new host as he said, "Never leave a public area with someone Douglas unless you are absolutely sure you know them!" I nodded and stopped in my tracks and just bowed my head and thanked God. "If it hadn't been for your friend, I would not have known where you were!"

I asked him what he meant.

He said, "I didn't catch his name, but said, 'You know, your friend who brought me to you!' I told him I didn't have a friend with me. He said, "Then who is..." he looked behind him where the tall Brazilian had been standing while we spoke. I looked for him too, but we couldn't find him. I told Aristarchus I thought the tall dude was HIS friend and he said, "No Douglas, I arrived here alone, and I'm sorry I was late! He came and said to hurry and he would introduce me to you!"

We looked at each other for a few moments...trying to take in what had just happened. Aristarchus looked at me. "Douglas, how did he know where you were? And how did he know to come get me and bring me to you?"

In that instant the realization of what had just happened hit us at the same time and we hugged each other and began praising God. I had just been delivered from real harm by a good looking sharp chinned Angel of the Lord...

I truly believe that.

****

Do you think God is not aware of what is going on in your life? Do you think he doesn't know your situation, the danger you may be in or the struggle you are facing? Do you not think God, the Lord of the Universe doesn't know the plans He has for you?

Let me tell you this my friend, God cares about your destiny, He cares about your future plans and He wants to work beside you to see it come to pass.

He hears your prayers...

He HEARS you.

He is always watching you and watching out for you. He wis watching over His word to perform it.

He hasn't stopped my friends...and they are there for you! God will make good His promises over your life. The prophecies He has spoken though His prophets will come to pass... though they tarry wait for them... be patient... God will fulfill His words over your life.

I will stand at my guard post and station myself on the ramparts. I will watch to see what He will say to me and how I will answer my reproof. Then the LORD answered me:

"Write down this vision and clearly inscribe it on tablets, so that he who reads it may run. For the vision AWAITS FOR THE APPOINTED TIME; it testifies of the end, and will not lie. Though it lingers, wait for it, SINCE IT WILL SURELY COME AND NOT DELAY...." Habakkuk 2:2

Waiting at the Car Wash...

There are a lot of things to do on days off.

Laundry. Cleaning and the one thing I only get to do maybe, 5 times, a year is get my car completely cleaned, inside, *and* out. This is not one of those "stop and get gas and…oh, by the way, "do you want a car wash?" questions at the gas pump.

Oh no…this is the dipsy doodle of car washes…the Grand Poobah of car washes, the "vacuum the rubble and scrub it with bubbles" car wash of washes. And it isn't just running it through an automated wash…oh no. This wash takes an hour and fifteen minutes where they clean the floor mats, vacuum between the seats, vacuum out the A/C vents, deep clean the leather seats and polish the tires.

You buy popcorn for this kind of car wash and then sit under a shaded area to watch 5 people crowd around and into your vehicle to polish the paint. Moisturize the leather seats. Lovingly clean your wheels and use little bitty brushes to get in between the buttons on your dashboard. By the time they're done, you have a ride that Mario Andretti would be proud to drive.

After paying, I went outside to sit and watch the 20 or so employees polishing other vehicles and taking tiny brushes around the rims or tires making everything gleam. At first I went and sat way down on rows of benches, but I have to talk…it's a sickness with me.

I have to have someone to talk to about something…anything. So I moved from being a loner to a bench where a young woman was sitting. I asked if I could sit and she kindly said yes. It was a better seat, and I could see my car smile at me in anticipation of getting all scrubbed up.

I looked at the woman and asked, like a proud parent standing at the window of the nursery in a hospital, "Which one is yours?"

She kind of giggled at me and said, "You're really into this aren't you?"

I laughed. "It was a rare that I ever spent much money on my car, but when I did, I tended to go overboard."

I learned that her name was Sarah. She smiled broadly and said it was rare too, but she and her husband were so busy, that this was the only time she had to do it. I asked what kept them so busy. She said her husband was the worship pastor at a church in Thompson Station, not far from Brentwood.

I was thrilled because I loved worship and she was so excited about it. She told me about her children…and one in particular. She said, "We have a special needs child and sometimes he takes more attention than the others, but how happy he is!"

I was curious about that so I asked her. "Is it hard for you?"

Referring to having a special needs child when everyone around them had lots of children with no special needs whatsoever. Her 30 something eyes narrowed as she spoke.

"I fell in love with him when he was born right away. He can't speak, and is challenged to communicate with us, but his eyes tell me the whole story when I look into them…" her voice spoke tenderly as she imagined his image in front of her while we spoke.

A smile came upon her face.

She looked at me squarely, "Travis opens people to the love of God by looking and smiling at them… he communicates acceptance, friendship and God's love."

I discovered that she and her husband were going on a short trip together just to have some alone time. Her mother and father were coming in to take care of their children. I asked if she worried about Travis while she was gone.

"I worry about them all!" she said, "Travis is the one I least worry about. He picks daisies and brings them to me, to my husband and he'll pick them for my mother, too. He gives daisies to EVERYONE!"

She laughed out loud…

"He picks SO many flowers…he's my flower child!" She told me she wanted to do more in ministry and I asked her if I could pray for her.

She bowed her head. "Lord, I ask for my new friend that you would give her the desire of her heart to do something in ministry that will be useful and meaningful. I ask that she would be used to do exactly what Travis does…to communicate acceptance, friendship and God's love."

As if on cue, over the car wash speakers came her name…I stood and gave her a daddy hug. She thanked me for the prayer and one of the workers cleaning her vehicle came over and asked her to come look at her car. We waved goodbye with promises to keep each other in prayer.

It took another 30 minutes or so for my little Solstice to get finished, but finally the speaker blurted out my name and I went walking toward the car. The guy who was showing me the vehicle proudly walked me around it. I thanked him and gave him a really good tip. I've worked in service industries and you need to always tip people as MUCH as you can afford to tip…it is really how they make their living.

As I went to open my door and get in, I broke out into a huge smile. Before she had left, she had found a moment to gather from the trash can one of three dozen daisies that had been cleaned out of her car and placed the prettiest one on my driver's seat. Travis had touched me and made me smile without ever having met him. God savors the gifts that other people throw away.

Sarah had known Travis was a Down Syndrome baby before she gave birth to him, but determined not to throw him away. And, out of the trash she had chosen one of her sweet boy's precious daisies and rescued it from the trash so it could bring another person joy.

I have pressed it in a book at home to always remember that God doesn't make trash…he gives beauty for ashes, the oil of joy for mourning and a boy with smiling eyes to communicate His love—

PERFECTLY!

How I Became Stupid...

Note to my readers: God interrupts our lives and intervenes long before we ever recognize Him. The following two stories are when I recognize that He reached into my world and used people to reshape and prepare my life. I hope you will begin now, to look into your past for when God reached into your early life to prepare you…

I was never a great student although I tried hard especially in Math class. But try as I may, I never really seemed to get a lot of the concepts right. I just didn't like it. My personality was always to look outside and think about being with other people. I was such a social child, that; to me, everything else in school just seemed to get in the way of talking with people, laughing with people and interacting with others.

I knew that it was important to learn reading, and spelling and geography, and I did those pretty well, but I always wanted to "cut to the chase" and get out and be around people. That was what I liked, because I was good at making friends and influencing people! *(Apologies to Dale Carnegie).*

I don't want you to interpret what I am saying as "learning isn't important" because I am not saying that. But I recognize that the model of every student doing the same work as every other student, was not one that suited me.

The content of the classes was very important, but the way I learned was in short bursts, not long class lectures and repetition. It bored me, and quite honestly, when a young boy gets bored, he acts out.

Sometimes they cause trouble, sometimes they talk, or make jokes, or fiddle around with things in their desks. I did ALL of the above. And my teachers weren't quite sure what to do with me.

At times, I was told to go to the principal's office, other times I was given the assignment of writing 100 times on the blackboard, "I will not talk during class". I got pretty good at that one, although my parents did not like having to pick me up after school because I had missed the bus.

I understand their frustration with me. The teacher was trying to teach 35-40 kids and here was this "troublemaker" frustrating their best efforts. I wasn't a bad kid; I was just bored and couldn't concentrate for long periods of time.

For a while, I think the faculty thought I would learn my lesson, but it stretched into years. I got up in the morning dreading school, and not because I didn't want to learn, but because I knew that the little gremlin inside of me that wanted to socialize would get the better of me sometime during the day and I would get in trouble. I really liked my teachers and wanted to please them especially from first through third grades.

In about 4th grade, my teacher took it to a new level…she began publicly humiliating me and man, did she have an arsenal of weapons! Many times I would walk into the classroom and smile and say, "Good morning Mrs. ----" and she would roll her eyes as if to say, "it was until *you* got here!"

There were times she would say, "Okay, let's see if even Doug can answer this question!" I felt my face turning red and got sick to my stomach. When I would raise my hand when she would ask a question to the entire class, she would look and me and say, "put your hand down, I want a good answer!"

On one particular day, when I answered a question correctly and expected to get an "attaboy", she said, "well, what do you know, he got one right!" to the laughter of all my classmates.

Later after school, she said, "You know Doug, I was wondering, does dumb run in your family?"

I had been taught that the teacher was always right. My parents had raised me to believe what adults said was true, and so in answer to her question and in a broken voice I recall saying very quietly, "I guess so."

And, the die was cast…

I was stupid and everyone knew it. That night on the bus, I didn't look forward to going home and getting on my bike. I walked through the woods and cried my eyes out. Here I was at 9 years old, and I was stupid, and it must be true because my teacher had told me so. My parents didn't really know what was wrong. I just changed. I became sullen and angry.

****

Over the next two years, I would like to say that I buckled down and got with her program, but instead, I declared war. She would say, "Everyone back in class after recess at 11:30!"

I would walk in at 11:35. She would assign a punishment, I would smile and say, "Is that all?"

She would glare at me and I would smile and say, "How about something really hard?"

"Is this all you have for me?"

This brought me to the attention of the principal, who, knew my parents and called them in. I would like to say, I got to tell my side of the story, but instead I got in more trouble at home. I feigned being sick so much that, even when I really was sick, my "cry wolf" routine fell on deaf ears. I hated myself, because I had no brains, and going to school just underlined that very clearly.

When I entered Jr. High, (that's middle school for you Millennials), a less structured learning style came to my rescue. I was thrilled to have shorter classes and the opportunity to leave the classroom between classes, meet people and go to another class. My grades and attitude improved greatly. My homeroom teacher was a young pretty woman named Cindy Miller.

Mrs. Miller was a diminutive woman, with glasses and very keen discernment. Many times she would gently talk to me when I would be unruly. She never tried to embarrass me.

When passing her in the hallway between classes, I recall she would come across the hallway just to say hello to me. My hard shell began to crumble, but the deeply ingrained habit of not doing my work, was still alive.

One day, when I had not done my lessons, Mrs. Miller sent a runner to the gym where I was at basketball practice, with a note to my coach. He told me she wanted to see me in the reading lab. I figured I was in trouble.

When I walked in, she was angry with me, because I had promised to do my work and had simply broken my promise. She told me to get in "push up" position for punishment and I obliged. However, unlike my elementary school teacher, Mrs. Miller did something no one had ever done.

She knelt down next to me and began to weep. "Doug, you are so smart, and you have so much talent, how can I help you sweetheart?" She was appealing to me. "I hear your answers in class, and they are so smart, and you analyze things so well. And every teacher I talk to likes you and they say you are a natural leader, but you seem bent on destroying yourself!" Tears were streaming down her face. She asked the question of questions… "Who told you that you were stupid?"

There it was!!!!

It was the question that unlocked 8 years of falsehoods that I had believed about myself. I could not stand it any longer and at 14, I began to cry like a baby right there in her reading lab on the floor.

She took me in her arms and cradled me while I wept all the while telling her of what had happened for years. It felt as if for the first time, someone finally believed me! Oh, just to hear those words.

"Doug you are so smart…."

They wiped clean the blackboard written with 10,000 sentences that read, 'dumb runs in my family'. I thought, "She knows…she really knows that I'm not dumb!" I was a mess. Snot, and tears, and drooling and crying so hard I couldn't catch my breath….I called it "machine gun" crying.

For a moment I felt like I was going to get caught crying by my friends, but we were alone in that lab, and she just kept repeating, "You are not dumb, you are not dumb, you are not dumb!"

She changed it to "You are so smart, you are so smart, you are so smart!" That made me cry more, because I had NEVER had the audacity to believe something like that.

She took my face in her hands and said, "Doug, you don't have to learn like anyone else, talk like anyone else, or BE anyone else….you just be you. I like who you are!"

Today, in a politically correct world, we have removed that humanity from our teachers, but Cindy Miller was no straw woman. She was little, but she had tough love, and her tears were the key to healing my wounded soul.

She became my personal cheerleader while I was in Jr. High School. She would walk up to me between classes and ask how my classes were going with genuine interest. She was my school mom.

****

By 9th grade I was averaging a B+ in about every class. I left Jr. High School without ever saying goodbye to her and have never seen her again.

On my first day of High School, I remember walking into the main hallway and trying to find my homeroom like every other sophomore. Upon finding my room, I walked in to find many of my Jr High School classmates in the same homeroom.

The homeroom teacher began calling roll, and when he came to my name, he stopped and held up a note and said, "This is a message for you". I thought it might be from my parents, but it was a sealed envelope with beautiful penmanship with my name on it.

I went back to my desk and opened it, without anyone looking. There, on the paper was a singular line written, with the words, "Smart runs in your family!" Good luck Doug!"

It was signed by Cindy Miller.

My First Encounter with Mercy...

At the age of five, my parents announced to me, that is my mother announced to me, that unfortunately she would need to go to work. The economic necessities of raising a small brood such as ours in the Sixties demanded that more money come in.

Not only was her going to work due to the cost of living, but the cost of sending four children to a private Catholic school meant that my care would now need to fall to my maternal grandparents who lived not a quarter mile down the country road upon which we lived.

Maynard and Ann Martin had raised 7 children in the middle of the depression.

My mother, the eldest was reared on that small farm in Bartholomew County and now, in the same home where she grew up, I was to be watched after until such a time as I would go to school. I remember not knowing what to do when I first arrived after my parents dropped me off in the morning.

My grandparents were old … I mean…they were OLD and here I was this kid, ready to pounce on any fun I could find. In terms of doting grandparents…they were not the most affectionate but I don't say that in a mean or resentful way. I can't explain exactly why it was, but as a small child I was extremely affectionate. I would crawl up on a visitor lap to our home and hug them.

My parents a bit embarrassed by this would mumble something to the person and peel me off their neck and place me back on the floor. Like a monkey, I would crawl right back up into their laps.

In hindsight, I now understand…and you who are reading this probably won't, but, well…I was born a gentle soul. Don't get me wrong, I can be a real butthead when I want to be, but I just was BORN with this capacity to care for people. It was written on my soul somewhere before time began. I came out of the womb and wanted to hug and to love and to kiss and to care for.

I was a hugging fool.

It is amusing to me now, that the visitors to our home would finally submit to my hugs and whether they liked it or not they left knowing that someone in that house really liked them. It makes me laugh as I write this about myself.

Again, I'm saying nothing bad about my grandparents, they just weren't the huggy type. They were farmers, pure and simple. They had things to do and places to go and cows to look after and wood to chop. I recall my grandmother telling me to get outside and find something to do. So much for picking blackberries and getting a tan like my mom used to do when she watched me during our summers together..

My grandfather was a truly kind man. He would whistle all day as he worked. He always was working, always busy. He raised rabbits, which I thought was great. What a great guy to raise all these rabbits just to pet and to hold!

That is, I thought it was really great until I saw why he raised rabbits. They weren't for cuddling, they weren't for petting, they were for killing, skinning and taking to the market to sell.

My grandparents didn't have a lot of rules for me to follow, but the ones they had were to be obeyed. The day came when I was unable to resist the one rule I had been given in my grandparents' house.

That rule was, I was not; under any circumstances, allowed to go into the basement. The stairway that led down into the very dark musty basement was narrow, with stairs that were rickety and there might even be bugs down there.

For me, however, it was a deliciously tempting cavern in which I knew pirates and robbers lived. I had always seen the door which lead to the basement, but opportunity for opening it had never presented itself until one day.

My grandmother had finished washing clothes and had wrung them out on the old fashion wringer that was on the top of her washer. It was an electric wringer though…not a hand cranking wringer.

Anyway, she had just finished wringing the laundry and had gone outside to hang the laundry on the clothesline. Now was my chance.

I quietly opened the door, held on to the handrail for dear life and walked down into the darkness of the basement. Step by step I got closer and closer to the cement floor at the bottom.

Upon reaching it, the smell of old musty moisture filled my nostrils and my eyes adjusted to the darkness. I could see a string hanging down from a light bulb on the ceiling and reaching up I pulled on it. To my amazement, the light shone on shelf upon shelf of glass jars filled with all kinds of things. Tomatoes, peaches, even potatoes in jars with lids on them.

I was dumbfounded!

There were smaller jars on shelves that were lower that had stuff that looked like…well, like jelly. Over in the corner to my right was a record player unlike anything I had ever seen.

It had a handle on it that; when I wound it up like a toy, out of the big bell looking thing on the front of it would come music. Somebody singing a song about "Elmer's Tune". I stopped the turntable from playing anymore music because I didn't want to be discovered.

When I put my hand out to stop it, the turntable resisted and the edge of the record cut me slightly. I reacted by pulling back my hand and when I did, I knocked against the shelf that held the jars of vegetables and jellies. All of a sudden, "smash!!!" one of the jars fell on the concrete floor and smashed to smithereens. Letting go of the turntable, Elmer's Tune began playing at full volume.

Heavy footsteps were heard over my head. It was my grandmother walking to the top of the stairs.

My grandmother was a big woman. She wore old country dresses with black shoes that looked like they were bought from a men's store. The sound of those footsteps made me so scared that I bumped the shelf again and AGAIN another jar of jelly hit the dust.

****

"Dougie! (she called me Dougie) I want you to go out to the tree and cut me a switch."

For those of you who live in this politically correct, sanitized, 'don't spank my kid cause he's my buddy', age of timeouts let me help you to understand what 'cut me a switch' means.

It means that an intense lesson of life is about to take place. It means that your butt cheeks and not your ears are going to be the principle receptors of the lesson… probably with welts and your legs too, just because they are there.

'Cut me a switch', means you are going to remember this lesson and I guarantee you will NEVER forget it. In fact, you may be able to point to the scars forty years later and lie about where you got them to your fishing buddies.

It meant going to a tree with a knife, and cutting a green, willowy branch, maybe three to four feet long and about half the thickness of a pencil off the tree. Skinning it from any leaves and swinging it in the air until it made the sound of a whip.

Taking it to your grandmother whose eyes were bleeding with anger for you breaking two of her preserves she had stored for winter. She would instruct you to turn around and when you did, man…you would swear that Satan and his demons in hell had decided to burn you with fire at that moment.

You would try to run…but a strong, smart grandmother would already have you by the arm…and running around her in circles, she could keep it up in perfect syncopation until you snot cried and snorted and couldn't catch your breath, this is what was in store for me.

I would not look up…I simply obeyed. But instead of getting a green, willowy, switch from the tree, I looked for the puniest, most rotten, ready to fall apart stick I could find and brought it to her.

By the time I returned with the stick, (which, I milked for a LONNNG time) the blood in her eyes was gone, and when I presented my pitiful excuse of a switch, (I think I saw a flashing smile come on her face then immediately disappear…it looked like it couldn't hurt a fly) she told me to hold onto the chair in front of me.

I remember holding that chair and visibly shaking.

Here it comes! What will it read on my gravestone? "Here lies a grape jelly waster!" What will my family say?

"If only he had listened to Grandma," my sister, would say.

"We told you he was an orphan," my brothers, would say.

At that moment, standing between heaven and hell, I heard what I believed was my grandmothers wind up. A mix between the sound of a tornado and hurricane ready to blow me to bits. Instead, I heard my grandmother sniffing and weeping.

At this moment of expected pain, I instead felt the brush of my grandmother's hair against my cheek and she was crying as she placed a kiss on my face. "Dougie, I want you to remember that while you were found guilty in the middle of your sins, Christ died for you…you deserve punishment, but from me, you will get only what I received, Mercy."

With that, she broke the stick over her knee, took me in her arms and held me while she cried her eyes out. I began crying too.

I WAS guilty. I WAS a sneaking jelly thief.

I had raided the stores of food, and now the colony would starve in the cold winter. I had scratched "Elmer's Tune" and I deserved not only the stocks, but to be executed at musket point in front of the village elders.

During that moment of unexpected reprieve from the Governor, I realized that my own mothers' propensity to be forgiving had come from this saintly old lady in combat boots. She was all toughness on the exterior, but she had a better understanding of her own need for mercy than her need to mete out punishment.

I cried with my grandmother because it was the first, the earliest recollection I would have of God's mercy on my life.

What relief! There would be other times, even life-threatening times in my future, where I WOULD receive the justice side of the law…but for that day, the sweetness of forgiveness stung much greater than any switch that I would have cut.

I am 58 today as I write this, and I can tell you with certainty, that I feel it as surely as if it had just happened to me. Such is the effect of being forgiven. Once you have received it, you never, ever forget it.

Thanksgiving 2010

It was mid-November in 2010 when I stood outside on the curb of the dealership where I worked and surveyed the scene before me. Snow had lightly dusted the lot and I brushed it off of the windshields of every car to prepare for the days business.

A small breeze blew and I pulled my coat around my face with one hand and brushed with the other. I groaned. I had seen better days. I had lived in South America and had been involved in ministry years before, and; on days like this, the sweetness of those days…having been used by God to change lives stung my heart a bit as I complained to God about my current state.

I complained a lot actually. I felt as though my life really didn't count for much. After going from job to job, I had lots of regrets and often complained to God that I wasn't doing anything to change people, nothing to improve the world, nothing but work and go home…day after day.

As the thoughts swirled in my head and my hands were approaching frostbite, a car drove onto the otherwise empty lot. It was a Sunday, which promised to be busy, but so far only me and one other salesperson were on staff.

Out of the car emerged a woman wearing a heavy coat and a scarf. Her eyes looked red and I guessed she was catching a cold. I approached her and said, "Not a great day to be out is it?"

She tried smiling, but kept her head down and mumbled a rather tired, "My daughter needs a car."

I invited her to come in and warm up at my desk. I poured her a cup of coffee and she gratefully accepted it. Dabbing her eyes again with a worn out tissue, she said, "My husband is coming also…we need to find a car for our daughter."

I smiled and asked a bit about the type and model of car she was looking for. As she began to describe the car, the door opened abruptly and in came walking a tall man without a coat and rubbing his hands together.

From the look she gave him I knew it was her husband. He nodded to me and began talking quietly to his wife. I gave them some privacy. Reappearing with another cup of coffee, I introduced myself to the man and he sat down next to his wife.

The showroom was completely empty with the exception of this couple. They sat silently. I thought that maybe this idea to buy a car for the daughter was not a mutual one.

The man, for his size, (I guess 6 foot 6 inches tall) looked haggard. He looked into his lap and his wife, continued wiping her eyes. The atmosphere became thick. I could tell there was a strain between them and I didn't want to interfere.

In an effort to give them time to talk a bit, I offered a private conference room, where we could talk about their daughter's car before going out on the cold lot to test drive one. They both appeared grateful for the opportunity to get out of the main showroom and get to a more private area.

I felt like an intruder, so I said, "why don't I give you both an opportunity to talk a bit, and I'll be back shortly?"

The husband spoke up. "No…no need sir, we…a," he was searching for his words. "My daughter was involved in a car accident that totaled her car."

I asked if she was alright. The mother blushed, and put her face into her hands, and this time I could hear her cry.

"Is everything alright with your daughter?" I hesitated to pry, but I had never been in this situation before. I waited at least 30 seconds for him to reply.

"Our daughter will be fine" he replied… "She is only 17 and," he paused, internally asking whether he should take me into his confidence. "We discovered while she was in the emergency room that she is pregnant."

The mother truly broke down at this point. I grabbed the box of tissues on the table, and was grateful for the opportunity to do something. Handing her the box, she acknowledged thanks and looked at me.

"I know this is not what you expected…you want to sell cars, and I'm so sorry to just break down like this."

As I sat back down in my chair, something happened. I can only describe it like, a smell of spring rain and a warm presence came physically into the room.

I heard myself say, "This is why I came to work today Mrs. ------."

She was surprised by my answer, as was her husband… AS WAS I!

A bold confidence came upon me, or I should say, welled up within me and a true love moved up from my stomach to my throat…it's the only way I can describe it.

The wife and husband both looked at me. There was no more talk of cars or features like cruise control or paint color. They looked at me expectantly, as if this was what they were waiting to hear.

I sat back in my chair and smiled. "You're thinking her life is over before it begins, aren't you?"

I asked.

"You're thinking she lied to you, maybe even disappointed you…" Tears formed on the eyes of the husband and his lip quivered. "She's scared because she loves you so much. She knows she made a terrible mistake."

An intense boldness came upon me, as if, I was the counselor they needed to hear from. I also began to weep but without fear. The presence of Jesus was in the room at that very moment.

As tears rolled down my cheeks, I explained, "Your daughter is so sorry for being impulsive and not trusting you to tell you…but she was afraid."

The father spoke up, "I know…I'm so hard on her, telling her she has to go to college, that she has to wait until marriage…I have been mad at her, and I'm sure she can feel it."

The mother also spoke up. "It's just that our family…our name in the community…" and then she stopped, feeling embarrassed.

I spoke up…"And you know she feels that shame, right?"

Again she broke down weeping.

I said, "Let me ask you a question, are you gonna love your daughter no matter what? Are you gonna love that baby? Will you be sitting on the front seat of the church in 20 years when your grandchild gets married and rejoice when they have THEIR first baby?"

The husband smiled, "I sure will!" he exclaimed beaming.

"Will you gather around your daughter and hug her and forgive her and then be thrilled as she walks through her pregnancy? Will you stand by her side in the delivery room? Will you let anything hurt her?"

The mother stood up. I thought, *Oh dear God, Doug, your big mouth! She is going to slap you…"*

"Nothing will hurt her!" she said it like an oath.

"What about the shame?" I asked… "What will your friends think?"

The father joined his wife by standing. "Our loving friends will love our daughter, so will her friends, so will our church….so help me God!"

Energy pulsed through the air. Whereas five minutes ago there was the depths of despair, resolute faith was now present. Discouragement slinked off and under the door. Where there was once only shame, there was now joy.

"And she wants to name him William!... It's a wonderful name "William" don't you think?!"

Her husband, William, agreed, and so did I. They were shouting in that room. They didn't care who heard them or what people thought of them…

"She's going to finish school and whatever she wants after that…we are going to help her!"

The couple embraced and wept and laughed and embraced. I felt a bit out of place, but they wouldn't let me leave the room. At that moment, the husband's cell phone rings. By the initial few words, I understood it was their daughter calling.

The father, overcome with emotion said, "Sweetie, everything is going to be fine. We love you so much!"

The mother was talking into the phone too. "I can't wait to go shopping for baby clothes honey!"

They were silent…and began weeping again…their daughter, overcome with love, was crying on the other end of the phone.

"It's okay honey…we're all gonna see this through together!" said her mother.

As quickly as it began, it was over. I stood and got hugs, handshakes and pats on the back…and all I had done was offer coffee and safety. As they walked back to their car and departed, I put my coat back on and started to walk out the front door when once again, I heard God speak to me.

"I place you where I want…and 20 minutes in an office with Me present will always do more than you standing alone behind a pulpit for 30 minutes."

The day was about over. As I walked to my car I realized Thanksgiving had come early this year on the car lot. He didn't need a theologian…God wanted an available car salesman. And there in my car, in November, I asked forgiveness for my complaining.

All I heard the Lord say was… "That's remarkable son…truly remarkable."

We Have to Engage...

Twice Daily is my favorite. I go in everyday to get my fix of chocolate milk. One quart, Purity brand. It was at Twice Daily that I was once misidentified as Taylor Hicks, which; I later discovered after looking up his most recent picture, wasn't a compliment unless I look like I weigh 350 lbs....

Today, I walked in and retrieved the aforementioned chocolate milk and went to stand in line. I was feeling festive. It's Friday, the last workday for me until well into the New year. I stood third in line from the cashier and decided to speak to the young woman standing in front of me.

"Good morning!" I said cheerfully.

She turned around and amazed me with a warm glowing smile.

I believe that we DO NOT live in a mean society, full of cynical people who are angry with the world. Rather, I believe we live in a society that desperately aches for genuine human contact where people speak kindly to each other.

The thing is, most young people today, don't know how to react to real kindness or how to carry on a conversation. They have not been prepared on how to respond to civil conversation between strangers.

Come to think about it, a lot of people in my generation have forgotten how to do it too.

"Good morning," she responded.

I asked, "Are you ready for Christmas? Do you have a lot of people to get gifts for?"

Surprisingly, she was ready for a conversation. She turned to respond, and as she did, I saw her profile. She was an expectant mother. Her little tummy pushing out...I smiled. I love young mothers. There is something so pure about a woman with child.

Especially at this time of year...she saw me smile, as she answered my question. "I only have two more to buy for" she said. "I don't like big crowds in stores." I agreed with her.

Now, I have been discipled by wonderful men and women of God over the years and I know from ugly experience… that a man is NEVER to even mention that he suspects a woman is pregnant unless he actually sees a child emerging from her body, but this little thing was about 28 years old or so and skinny as a rail and I just knew she hadn't just eaten an entire watermelon, so I took the chance.

"Okay…when are you due?" She smiled, I just loved that, she loved being asked about her baby.

"I am due on January 17th!" she said with excitement in her voice. I asked her if this was her first and she nodded yes. I could tell she was so excited about having her child…

I remembered those days long ago when my wife and I were awaiting our first born. Those days are halcyon days in my memory now, although back in the day, they were bustling with activity and concern over finances, baby clothes and preparations.

"Is it a boy?" She nodded.

"Men always ask if it's a boy!" We laughed.

I asked if she had a name picked out. She wrinkled her brow a bit. "My boyfriend and I can't decide on a name. We would like to name him something significant, something…different."

My mind immediately went to "Moon Unit" and "Dweezle".

The names of Frank Zappa's children. She said she didn't know who Frank Zappa was and I said, "Believe me, it doesn't matter!"

She studied me for a minute as the cashier was ringing up her purchase. Finally she asked, "do you know any names that are…significant?, special?" The cashier was now involved in the conversation and suggested a couple of names which were good ones. I thought it was odd no one else was standing in line. She turned her attention to me again.

"You know, it is no coincidence your child is coming during this special time of year. Since you know it's a boy, have you ever thought of the name, Christian?"

Her mouth opened wide and so did her eyes. "That IS a wonderful, unique name!" She kept saying, "Christian…hmmmm Christian."

I asked her if she had any names in her family she had been thinking about and she shook her head *no*. She kept saying, "Christian…wow."

As an afterthought, I told her I was sorry for not introducing myself. I told her my name and told her my wife and I had moved here about two years ago. I apologized for not asking her name.

"It's just plain old Mary…just Mary."

I told her my wife's name was Mary Ann, but I had begun laughing when she told me her name.

She and the cashier asked why I laughed and I said, "Come on you two! A young woman with child and her name is Mary!?"

They both laughed.

She said they weren't looking for a farm with a manger to deliver her child and we all laughed. I paid for my chocolate milk and thanked the cashier. "Merry Christmas!" I walked out with Mary and blessed her. "God Bless you Mary, and your baby and your boyfriend…and Merry Christmas!" She thanked me, wished me a Merry Christmas and got into her SUV and drove away.

I've thought all day about that exchange. I think the world wants to be approached in love. I think they want someone to be interested in them…I know I do. I believe they ache for the fruit of the Spirit, Love, Joy, Peace, Patience, Kindness, Goodness, Faithfulness, Gentleness and Self Control.

The Bible says, "against these, there is no law." There is nothing that can regulate the fruits of the Holy Spirit. And they are in genuine demand. I think it is a chip shot to love people into the Kingdom…**if we will only engage.**

Beginning at Four Years Old...

My mother belonged to The Doubleday Book Club, as a young woman, and every month new books would arrive at our small Indiana home. With excitement she would open the boxes to see what titles she had received. My mother loved to read and read to me every chance she got. Every book that would arrive, she placed on the bookshelves in our living room.

Among the titles were such books as, *A Bell for Adano, A Farewell to Arms*.

One book in particular that a four-year-old loved. It was a picture book; actually, a travel book filled with black and white pictures from countries around the world entitled, "Around the World in a Thousand Pictures."

Since I could not read, I loved taking the book down and looking at the pictures. Page after page of scenes from all over the world spread out before me. And of course, not knowing what I was really looking at, I had no idea that these were pictures of Italy, France, England... photos from all over the world.

Every day, I would look at the pictures and strangely enough, each time I would arrive at a *certain place in the book* I would call out to my mother and say, "Mommy, come and look at this picture!"

Dutifully, she would lovingly come in and I would point to the picture in the book and proudly announce, "That's where I will go when I grow up!"

She would smile and pat my head and say, "That's wonderful dear", and go back into the kitchen. I did this so much that the book would naturally fall open to the pages that I said were my favorites.

In time, I grew older and the book lost interest for me and was placed back on the shelf and then into a box in our basement where my parents placed old things that they would either throw away or give away.

I went to elementary school, middle school and then to high school where I became involved in sports and grew interested in girls. I received a scholarship to Indiana University where after the first semester, I was injured and left school. I moved to Kentucky and for a long time just drifted from job to job.

After a series of very miraculous interventions by the Lord, I found myself as a missionary to South America. This is where I now see that God was leading my life, because I could never have gotten to South America without going to Kentucky and would never have had the experience that I am about to relate to you.

One afternoon, as I was walking through Botofogo, a suburb in Rio de Janeiro, I was looking at the beautiful bay, filled with sailboats and at the beaches with their white sand and was thinking about what a wonderful thing it was that I was allowed to live there when I was suddenly stopped in my tracks.

Tears began to roll down my face and heaving sobs came over me. I couldn't speak, but I knew I had to get to a phone, and had a friend ask in Portuguese for the operator to place a collect call to my parents because I couldn't speak due to being so overcome with emotion.

When the call went through and my parents heard me sobbing and feared that something horrible had happened. "What's wrong Doug?" my mother asked.

I tried to speak over the sobbing and explain to her but I wasn't making sense. "Slow down, and tell me what is wrong!"

I slowed my breathing, gathered my emotions and said to her. "Mom go look on page 23 in 'Around the World in a Thousand Pictures,' she said she would later," but I explained to her, "the very picture that I looked at when I was four years old…it…" my voice broke again. "I am looking at it right now!"

There in front of me was Sugar Loaf Mountain. I hadn't known the name of it and I hadn't connected the dots that it was pictures of Brazil that I had looked at as a child. It was a God coincidence. I had gotten a preview of this very moment at four years of age.

My father was on the extension phone and had gone to the basement to find the book. He found it and got back on the phone and said, "It is Sugar Loaf Mountain on page 23, Doug…I see it."

My mother began to weep softly. My dad, who was very Latin and whose first impulse was almost always to get angry blurted out, "will one of you tell me what the hell is going on?"

My mother said, "It's the picture that Doug used to show me when he was four years old...he would point to that very page and tell me, 'Someday I am going to that Country'."

For 10 seconds or so there was silence on the phone. Mom and I knew that a four-year-old boy had seen 20 years into the future, and that my being in Brazil was no coincidence. The God of the Remarkable had shown up.

I spent four and a half years in Brazil helping to establish two churches. I baptized dozens of young Brazilians in the ocean and lived an adventure I couldn't have dreamed possible.

My eyes were open with this experience about how God had given me insight as a child as to something he wanted me to do and as I looked back throughout my life, I began to see puzzle pieces that fit into place in other events and I immediately recognized that none of the things that had happened growing up were coincidence.

****

How can I convince you that God is constantly moving, taking action on your behalf to position you in a place where you will not only see Him change lives, but also to USE you to do it?

Listen, I am a nobody, born to a lower middle-class Hispanic/English/Irish family from Indiana. I have had no special training to do and see the things I have seen. The only explanation that I have is that the God of the Remarkable is seeking to reach into the earth to change lives and I was available. I can't even take credit for that.

Stop and consider incidents from your past that made you curious about God. Was it a relative? A friend who influenced you. A teacher perhaps who showed you so much love that you wanted what they had? Was it a book you picked up? My friend, it was the God of the Unremarkable showing up to interrupt your life.

He was moving in your life from the time you stepped out of the womb. Scripture says: *"For it is God who works in you to will and to act in order to fulfill his good purpose."* Philippians 2: 13

In Jeremiah it says: *"I knew you before I formed you in your mother's womb. Before you were born I set you apart and appointed you as my prophet to the nations."* Jeremiah 1:5

Lunch Box Messages

I remember the first day of school. It was a tiny classroom in a little parochial school in my little hometown of Columbus, Indiana. I remember the first song I learned at 6 years old.

"God is love, and he who abides in love, abides in God, and God in Him."

That is a different narrative than most children will have about their first day of school I think. Back in the sixties, growing up Catholic was a lot different than it is today. Yes, I mean it was much more God centered. In fact, I credit the Catholics for planting the seed of love for God in my heart.

As far back as fifth grade, I remember a priest visited our classroom with a filmstrip, (See antiques and ancient machines for the meaning of "filmstrip") with background music of The Fifth Dimension's song, *Up, Up and Away* playing telling about a group of people going too far away countries sharing the gospel with them. They were called Trinity Missions. On that day, in my fifth grade heart, I remember saying to myself, "That's it! I'm going to become a priest and become a Trinity Missionary!"

Then there was a young priest whose name I forget, who came to our religion class in sixth grade trying to tell us about this thing called "Christian Music" that he listened to. He brought a record, (see vinyl record to understand on "Bing" to understand what a vinyl record is) and while it played he furiously scribbled the words on the blackboard, (See old-time methods for teaching for "Blackboards). I can remember to this day how unique it was that someone had written a song and it wasn't a hymn or a Catholic song:

Sunday morning, very bright I read your book by colored light that came in through the pretty window pictures.
I visited some houses where they said that you were living,
And they spoke a lot about you and they talked about you giving,
They passed around a basket with some envelopes
I just had time to write a note,
But all it said was, "I believe in you."

Hymn by Songwriters: James Mason / Karen Gold / Noel Paul Stookey. Hymn lyrics © Warner Chappell Music, Inc

This was a song performed by a modern folk group Peter, Paul and Mary and it so impressed me that I got something in my throat and my eyes began to well up with tears and I didn't know why. I quickly tried to stifle the feeling and to keep my eyes from watering but there in that room in that early bud of my life, God reached into a classroom and stamped his name on my heart and staked His claim for this real estate.

This narrative is stuff and nonsense to anyone who really understands "grown up" eschatology. (See "speculative arguments among "learned" Christians about what God says about the end days".) Of course, God wouldn't speak to a little Catholic boy. How much blasphemy is that! Fact is, God has been after me ever since I was in the womb and on good days and bad days, He is still using any method to get my attention and He is doing the same thing with you.

Have you ever heard that special song that plays at the perfect time, maybe when you are sad, or when you needed to hear it, and it lifts you up and you say to yourself, "Wow, what a coincidence! I really didn't know what I needed and that song played at the perfect time!" How about when you hear someone speak and you feel inspired and begin to tear up and you say, "Man, that moved me!" Those "Aha" moments are exactly what those early memories did in me.

As I was placing price tags on merchandise at my favorite Big Box store yesterday, I was surprised when something came to my mind and all I can say is I literally felt the presence of God down on that floor with me while I was peeling stickers. He got right down with me, and made me to remember how He had gone to so many lengths to show me His love, to show me who He is and what He thinks of me.

Again, tears flowed on that cement floor in this hardware store in Brentwood Tennessee. I am not the most holy person. Not at all. I cuss when I hit my finger, I get impatient when the fast food line doesn't move fast enough and I get tired of endless political chatter on television. But that doesn't stop the Lord. He just insists on showing this former Catholic boy filmstrips in my mind about how He has clothed and fed and housed me for 62 years and I just don't understand why He would waste so much time on a mediocre believer!

In church on Sunday, my pal Mike Spencer; a bass player who doesn't even live here in Tennessee says during worship he tears up and it so touched me because that happens to me all the time. I think something inside of us as humans feels the atmosphere of heaven at times and it so moves us that we long for the completion of it. We long to enter fully into God's presence. It reminds me of the words of a different Catholic song I learned as a child:

I saw raindrops on my window,
Joy is like the rain.
Laughter runs across my pain,
Slips away and comes again,
Joy is like the rain.

Sometimes, I have to admit the pain of separation from God is deeper than that of a child who is stolen away from his mother at birth but carries with him a sense of loss that he can't name. I know what that is like. We have been stolen from our mother…all of us, and carried into an evil country. But somehow, someway, she continues to send us messages in our lunchboxes that say, "I'm here, and I'm watching you…I love you…here's a special song for you today…here is your favorite sandwich." We look around but we can't see her, but she sees us.

That is what it is like for God. He is sending you signals secretly into this world so you will know you are not alone. He will bring you through a friend your favorite ice cream, or make you your favorite meal, JUST FOR YOU, as you go through your day. His joy is like the rain…it falls and waters your life, and then, it's gone, only to fall again on another day. Joy is like the rain. And while this little foolish blog may not mean much to you today, it is proof that the reason God has given me a good memory is to recall all of his lunchbox messages over the years that I have tucked away for that day, when; I finally see my mom coming for me in our family car, to reveal to me for the first time her lovely face and to say, "Here I am!!!" On that day I get to hug her for the first time and thank her for all of the lunchbox messages.

I love lunch box messages.

I Almost Messed Up

I meet a lot of different people in my job at my favorite big box hardware store. It can be easy to go to two extremes for me… socialize with all of the people who come into the store and engage them in conversation which, would be MY choice. Or focus on my work and consider the non-stop requests for assistance as an Indiana sweat bee circling my head as I try to swat them.

You're probably thinking, *If I don't like the job, move on*, but, I genuinely DO love people and I think of the job as the nuisance and the people like the bright spot in my day.

Except for today, it was challenging.

I was up on a ladder today doing inventory on some chandeliers that are hung up on the lighting aisle when the guy approached my ladder to ask me for help. I had heard him walking down the aisle long before he got to me…cursing and talking to someone on his phone. It was a good thing I heard him before he got there, because I had a feeling there was going to be trouble, so I held on to the ladder as his voice approached.

Arriving at the location where I was perched; instead of saying "Excuse me!" he decided to shake the ladder at its base and shout, "HEY!" in order to get my attention.

At 6' 2", being over 8 feet off the ground with concrete as the floor, the prospect of falling is not a good one. I was a gymnast as a kid at 18 but there would be no graceful dismount from this height and…by the way that was 42 years ago!

Holding on tightly, I turned my head in his direction and scowled. I was not inclined to be friendly to a 40 something guy who was cavalier with my safety. Instead of, "What can I do for you?"

I came down the ladder and stood face to face with him. In my younger and more foolish days, I would have thrown down…and job be damned, but I looked at him in the eyes and heard the quiet voice inside say, 'Self-control Doug…self-control…'

So, I said, "How can I help, sir?"

Expletives came pouring out of his mouth…"No employees anywhere…#@%&!...I need help!"

My inner smart ass said, 'You sure do dude!'

Asking him what he was looking for, he stated the item he needed, which; just happened to be directly behind him. I leaned to his left and fetched the item of the shelf behind him and handed it to him.

He cursed again…this time, evidently with joy (cursing with joy?), and said: "You must be Mr. Big Box Store himself" (no he didn't say "Big Box", he named the store). I asked if that was all he needed and he said, "Yeah, that's it…I guess you can scurry up your ladder and resume dusting!" As he turned to leave, he got a phone call and began cursing again as he walked toward the checkout.

In my experience, every time I have run into someone with a big temper, there has almost always been an opportunity to either get angry with them or just move in the opposite spirit.

****

This brought to mind another situation I was once in. I was approached while sitting in the cab of my truck at a stoplight by a guy with a clenched fist wanting to hit me because I was playing *Midnight Train to Georgia* in my truck and he thought I was smiling at his girlfriend to flirt with her.

When I listened patiently to him, he relaxed and ended up apologizing. I was grateful I kept my cool because I can be get irked to the point of just giving it right back to a smart mouth. I really have to use self-control.

****

As the man was walking out, it was time for lunch and I was going to the convenience store right in front of the Big Box store to get a big bottle of water. As I walked out of the convenience store with my water, I heard a guy cursing and looked up and saw the same guy kicking the tire of his car, and slamming the car door to open the hood of his car. His pinpoint cotton French cuffs had gotten dirt on them as he tried to twist the cable on his battery. Evidently, his battery was dead. Guess who he was parked next to?

ME.

This past Christmas I had gifted myself a battery jumper, that I carry in my back seat in my truck. Without asking permission, and seeing he was trapped in a prison of anger, I walked to my truck right next to him.

He looked at me, wondering what I was doing out next to HIS car and watched to make sure I didn't ding his car door with my truck door. He cursed again, this time slamming his fist down on the plastic cowl that was over his engine.

I took my jumper box, put it lightly on his fender, attached the jumper cables and said, "Go turn your key." All this time he had just looked at me…not saying a word. His car started immediately.

Getting out of his car, he looked at me smiling and said, "You must be a F@#%$! Angel, dude!"

I hate to say it, but I didn't even acknowledge his comment with a look, I just unhooked the jumper box from his car and walked back to my truck to put it away.

As I closed my door, I looked at him and he was quietly watching me. As I walked away, he shouted, "Hey, let me give you some money!"

I finally looked at him and said, "You are a very angry man…and you were shown a lot of mercy just now…you need to get to the bottom of your anger."

He walked toward me…and I figured, "Well Doug, you are going to get hit!"

Instead he said, "My wife left me…and took my 14-year-old daughter…"

Now that my paradigm was changed, I told him, "The very God you curse jumped your car today…and instead of cursing him, He can redeem your situation." I turned and walked away.

After arriving back in the store, I looked behind me and he sat quietly at the steering wheel of his car…just staring out of the windshield.

This is why the Lord gave us the Fruit of the Spirit…which I used very poorly, because I admit it, I was ticked off at this guy. But the Lord will use whatever meager offering we have to reach the dying in this world.

Moving in compassion is often accompanied by taking risks…

Someone is Bringing Firewood

When Christmas comes around, there is one thing that makes me feel rich and it isn't having a lot of money to buy gifts.

It's firewood.

I don't know where or when it began but, having firewood stacked is a comforting feeling for me. Perhaps it is some ancestral emotion I inherited from long ago, but there is something about a fire in the fireplace that tells me all is well and that we are safe.

You know what I'm talking about…right?

The crackling of the fire; the long light it casts at night when the lights are low, the glowing of the embers… they all provide a comfort that is very tangible. It makes me pull my sweetheart a little closer, smile a little larger and think a little deeper.

A fireplace makes me remember people and places, too.

The flames flickering brings back images of campouts long ago, visits to my favorite place in the world…Brown County State Park, and fire pits around which I, my wife and friends used to sit and laugh.

I remember building fires for my children to sit around when they were younger. A good fire draws people around it for warmth and while we are gathered we interact with one another.

In fact, after one has taken the requisite number of pictures of it, a fire becomes almost a "No Device Zone". People put away their phones to stare into the fire and make conversation…mostly about how they love a good fire, but sometimes they tell you something deep…they make a comment about a time long ago, or a loved one far away.

I began thinking about that tonight as I sat looking into the fire.

I remember snow falling for the first time in Tucson Arizona. Well, it was the first time for my children and little family. Living in the desert southwest, the last thing one has in the drawer are gloves.

But I remember my oldest son, Isaac, at only 4 or five, putting a pair of my white gym socks on his hands and going out to try to scrape up enough snow to make a snowball. I thought about times when, in northern Kentucky, where you DO expect snow to fall when it came down so deep and thick, that we could sled down a big hill and onto the frozen lake. Coming in with pink cheeks and frozen fingers to stand around the fireplace and warm up.

I remember skating in Columbus Indiana at Lincoln Park when the ice-skating rink was still without a roof and outside and how packed it would be. There was a constant fire going inside in the fireplace and we would eat handmade pretzels and hot chocolate around it.

I think there is another reason I am comforted by firewood. A big stack of firewood tells me there is a provision that has been made for my comfort. When I look at a cord of firewood… it tells me someone labored to cut, season, gather, and stack it in preparation of the time when it would be needed.

There was no firewood in the little stable near Bethlehem though. I wasn't there, but I'll betcha there wasn't.

It was a place the animals were fed and kept in stalls and no kidding, there were all kinds of poo on the ground, because…well, there just was. There may have been a lantern lit by Joseph or the owner of the stable where he and Mary were allowed to spend the night.

And, it was cold.

There was a star in the East, that shone brightly that night…but there was no music or bells, or a comfy bed. Mary did the best she could to make her newborn child comfortable; placing him inside of a feed manger lined with straw and lots of swaddling cloth.

Joseph most likely stood at or near the entrance of the little stable, keeping watch out over the landscape to protect his little family. He didn't know it was Christmas… no one did. He just knew it was cold, and dark and smelly and he most likely felt like a poor provider for his wife.

Maybe he looked out over the distance and could see into a home of the owner of that stable where a fire roared in the fireplace around which that family gathered. I'm sure he shook his head and wondered why this was the only place he could find and probably asked himself if the whole thing about this child had been real…an angel appearing, really? Mary miraculously pregnant?

In the distance, there were figures walking toward them. Joseph grabbed his staff and told Mary someone was coming. Taking his stand in front of the stable, the men drew closer and they were carrying a torch and had wagons behind them.

As they approached, one of them, spoke up, "We…excuse me sir, we were told that a child has been born."

Joseph would have just looked at them and asked them to repeat that and one of the others would have said. "Sir, we are shepherds and…" he would turn around to look at the other shepherds with him for moral support continue, "and, we were out with our sheep when something happened…"

Another shepherd would speak up…"An angel…it was in the sky and told us that a baby savior had been born and we were led to this place… I know it's crazy but we swear to you sir, we are not drunk."

Inside of Joseph something like a deep sigh stirred and almost instantly tears appeared in his eyes. It was true!!! This baby that wasn't his, WAS someone special! His breathing increased and his pulse began to race.

He asked, "Say that again…tell me what you just said again!" grabbing the first shepherd by the shoulders.

And so, the third shepherd repeated the story, but this time he added, "An Angel of the Lord appeared to us, and the glory of the Lord shone around us, and we were terrified. But the angel said to us, 'Do not be afraid. I bring you good news of great joy that will be for all the people. Today in the town of David a Savior has been born to you; he is the Christ… whom you have been waiting for…THE LORD!'"

Inside of the stable, the baby whimpered and his mother pulled a cloak over the mound of swaddling cloths wrapped tightly around the baby. Joseph looked into the eyes of the four or five men before him.

Around them were many of their sheep and of course the wagon. He turned to look inside the stable and his eyes met Mary's. She was grinning…ear to ear and shook her head as if to say, "Please let them come in!"

One by one they would come in and kneel before the manger. They smelled bad… weeks out in the open with sheep. Some of them looked at the face of the baby…taking it in like the once in a lifetime opportunity it was.

As they stood, they would perhaps bow or show honor to the mother and then exit. They set up a small camp right there…and for the first time in Jesus' life… as Kings and others from the East arrived to bring him gold, frankincense, and myrrh, the shepherds…the lowest of the low on the social ladder at that time did the one thing they knew they could offer.

Taking wood from off their wagon…they built a fire to bring comfort and protection from the darkness.

****

Remember that even on the coldest of nights, when all the promises you have received don't seem true or when all of the prophecies made over your life don't look like they are ever going to happen, you are on the verge of a miracle. Someone somewhere is on their way to confirm the very thing God has promised to you.

It may seem that you have been led into a smelly and cold situation, but God's plans are designed to outwit the enemy and are not always understood by his children. He knows what you need, He has not forgotten you.

You are not hidden from God…He sees you wherever you are and He is coming!!! He is coming by the most unexpected way possible and just as a bonus; He is bringing firewood for you and for me!

The Hearts of the Fathers...

My children all live in different states. My eldest who today is 38, lives in Fairfax Virginia, my daughter, in the Queen City, Cincinnati, and my youngest son, on the west coast in Oregon. Suffice it to say that I miss my children on holidays and well, every day along with my grandchildren.

For those of you who are separated by distance from your loved ones, the ties that bind grow stronger over the holidays. Living in the Volunteer State, I admit to not seeing my children often and due to work, both mine and theirs, visits have to be planned in advance.

Those of you in the same situation as I, will understand when I say that seeing other families together fans the flames of familial love and makes the absence of my family even harder to bear at times.

Such was yesterday. I had gone to our neighborhood grocery to pick up some things and had just retrieved a cart (a buggy for those from the South… "No Ninos en la canasta!" for my Hispanic friends) and was walking into the produce aisle when I saw her.

The little girl with her mother was almost an exact copy of my granddaughter Genevieve. She had a tiny shopping cart that the grocery provides for children to walk alongside their parents to "play" shop.

Being the softie that I am, I stood back and watched as she would place an apple in her cart when her mother would stop to look at apples, and would clap when the auto sprinklers came on in the produce department to water the veggies.

My heart grew heavy with missing my little granddaughter and as they passed near to me, I looked at the little girl and into her cart.

"My goodness, you are being such a big helper to your mommy," I said looking her mother in the eye to make sure she knew I was a grandfather trying to be kind. She smiled broadly.

"Oh yes," she said, "she is my big helper!"

I got down on her level and asked her, "do you think you have enough room in your cart for cookies…I'm sure your mommy needs your help with that…"

I looked winking at her mommy who nodded. I produced two dollars and handed them to the little girl, who looked at her mother who said, "It's okay sweetie, you can take it."

These days with television news reporting atrocities of people kidnapping children and the reality that we live in a perverted and dangerous world; it was a refreshing thing that this mother understood I was simply trying to be kind.

As I looked behind the mother, there; standing by her side was an older woman, who I presumed to be either her mother or mother-in-law. The older woman made eye contact with me, looking me over carefully. When my eyes met hers, a smile broke out on her face.

She noticed my "Northern" accent, (which is no accent at all) and said, "You must be missing your grandchildren."

Admittedly, I confessed to her, "It's been too long…I have 5 that live on the coasts, but I have 3 locally that get hugged a lot!"

She asked about my grandchildren and I told her the names and ages of each one…a ritual that grandparents understand. Our encounter lasted no more than two minutes at the most, and probably less, then we all moved on to do our shopping. I waved goodbye to the little girl and walked on.

I gathered all the things I had been sent to purchase and got in line at the checkout. It was crowded for a Saturday evening, but I needed to get home for the big Titans game.

After paying and beginning to walk away, I heard the staccato sounds of little feet running toward me and the mother saying, "Sir?"

I turned around to seeing the little girl running toward me…grandmother in tow. I knelt down and she gave me a hug and held out for me a chocolate chip cookie. I got a little misty I have to admit and that's when the daughter spoke up.

"Sir, I wanted to thank you for your kindness…I am often so cautious about strangers," she paused looking at me to make sure I wasn't offended.

I nodded in agreement and said, "We live in a different world than when I grew up."

Her mother, close to my age, nodded.

The daughter said, "I am always watching when my children are in public for fear of the stories that I have heard on the news…but…" she paused looking down at her daughter. "I wanted to thank you for renewing my trust in strangers…my little one here told me when you walked away, 'He is somebody's grandpa and his grandchildren are looking for him… do you think he is lost?"

The young mother smiled at me and said, "Gretchen, my daughter; just wanted you to know she doesn't want you to be sad."

Well, of course, I became a tearful mess.

The mother said, "Wherever your children and grandchildren are…they should know you are a good grandpa…and have restored the faith of this cautious millennial in others."

At that the young mother, the older mother and little Gretchen gave me a hug. I melted. I thanked them for the kindness of saying something and heard little Gretchen say, as I walked out the door say to her mommy, "Maybe we should go looking for his grandchildren!"

****

I got into my car and just sat for a minute. I thought about my son turning 38 years old today…I thought about my daughter in Cincinnati and my son and his family on the West Coast… and said out loud, "How I miss you!"

I started the car and said a prayer, "Lord, watch over my family tonight…" I heard the Lord say, as I drove out of the parking lot and toward home, "Little Gretchen was your reminder that I always have you on my mind…and that I am watching over them."

I say this to grandparents everywhere…hold them all tightly…and kiss those precious little heads every chance you get. And, for young families everywhere, be mindful that kindnesses from older people toward their children may simply be the heart of the Father, reaching out to the children they miss. Thanks for the cookie…and especially the hug little Gretchen, and hugs to my five grandchildren who are so far away from me tonight…

Searching for Family from the Garden

I love the idea of a kindred spirit. Lucy Maud Montgomery's book, Anne of Green Gables was the first time I had ever read this phrase and it immediately struck a chord inside of me.

I am convinced that what each of us feel inside is unique only to ourselves, is actually shared by hundreds, thousands and millions of others across the world. I know this because of one distinct truth.

Whether or not you believe it; we share a common ancestry through our first parents Adam and Eve, and we are family. This human condition we hold in common, binds us together as the largest communal family in the universe.

It is because of this familial connection that; when one of us is down or worried or filled with hope, others of us can sense it. It isn't just a human condition; it is the spiritual tie that binds us together.

This is why yesterday, while taking quite a bit of time to answer the questions of a young couple about how to tile their entire house, I got a strong handshake from the young man and a short hug and kiss on the cheek from the young wife.

In that moment they were not my customers…I was helping two of my kids to tile their house by giving them the benefit of my experience and knowledge. I was their old dad, helping them out.

In fact throughout the days that I am working, I find myself listening more closely, and caring more about their projects than I used to do as a young man.

Later in the afternoon, a man approaches me about how to install blinds, a lady and her elderly husband ask about the best flooring for a kitchen and it's when I begin to ask questions that they hadn't thought about and come up with solutions that will fit into their budget, people seem to come alive.

I know it's an old and tired saying, but people don't care how much you know…..until they know how much you care. When they see in your eyes that you are taking time with them and that you don't think that people are an interruption in your day, it is then; that people will listen to whatever you say and take it to heart.

Yesterday there was a couple, not much older than 22 or 23 years old walking and trying to find the aisle for air filters. I saw the lost looks on their faces and since they were walking in my direction, I simply asked, "Okay you guys", (that is a Northern idiom, meaning…Okay you guys), "what are you looking for?"

The guy looked at me and kind of sheepishly asked, "Where are the things that you put in front of your furnace that catches all the dust and lint and stuff?" I smiled and genuinely tried not to laugh, but I was unsuccessful.

"You mean air filters for your furnace?" A big smile popped onto his face…"Yes, I guess that IS what they are…air filters!" Instead of pointing to the aisle, I began to walk them down to the right area. "What size are you looking for?" I asked.

"The young woman looked at me and asked, "Size…you mean there are different sizes?"

We arrived at the correct aisle and when they saw the hundreds of filters, she laughed out loud and said, "Well, okay, yes there are different sizes!"

We all three laughed and I asked if there was anyone at their home to go and snap a picture of the filter in their furnace and she frowned…as did he.

"No, but we don't live far away…can we go back really quick to see and come back?"

I told them of course, but then the young man said, "but…well, when we come back, a …" his young wife finished his sentence, "Will you be able to help us again?"

I can't tell you why…but the feeling of being needed flooded my soul with thankfulness and I nodded yes with a big lump in my throat. They left quickly and I headed back over to the flooring department where a woman stood in the tile aisle looking at a big stack of tile.

I never just say "May I help you.." which I abandoned years ago because, if I work somewhere, I had better be able to help them! So I said, "Hi…what is your project?" the lady looked at me with big eyes that said, "Oh thank God…someone is here!"

She grabbed my arm and said, "Please, tell me what to do!...I am doing something called, "flipping a house" and I was told by my husband to go and find some tile!"

I'm not a judge…okay? I don't want to make sweeping judgments against people because I don't like being judged myself, so I refrain from asking myself judgmental questions like, "where is her husband if he is flipping this house and why did he send her here without explaining what to look for and"

I stopped myself and just laughed and said, "This is gonna be so easy your husband is going to feel ashamed he doesn't know as much about tile as you do when we are finished!"

For the next 15 minutes, I asked what size the rooms were, and to my surprise she had a copy of the blueprints of the house on her phone. We began to design every room in that house, right down to the color of thinset and grout.

We built her shower and she was furiously taking notes and asking the difference between modified thinset and regular and large format tile thinset. She asked how to grout and I showed her how to hold the float. Just as that moment up walked the young couple who had gone in search of their air filter size.

"Hi Mr. Doug…we're back!" (I get called Mr. Doug because my name appears in big bold letters on the front of my apron.) I was almost finished with the lady "flipping" her house, but she immediately grabbed my right arm and said, "HE'S MINE!"

The young man and woman grabbed my left arm and said, "NO HE ISN'T, HE'S OURS…WE FOUND HIM FIRST!"

At this point I understood what a wishbone must feel like when two people are tugging at it from both sides…I was gonna get broken! I laughed but neither of them did.

So, I said, "Okay…ma'am, I DID tell them I would help them when they came back, but it is just for an air filter!" The house flipping woman said, that's fine, but I am walking down with you so that afterward we can come back and finish.

Down the main aisle we walked, the house flipping woman holding my right arm and the young couple holding my left. I had employees of my favorite big box store looking at me, thinking they were trying to help me walk!

One even came up to me and said, "Doug, are you okay?!" with genuine concern. The young couple said, "Oh no, we are making sure Mr. Doug helps us and we are not going to let him go until he does! The house flipper nodded in the affirmative as well.

The employee laughed and told them, "Other people work here you know… we can all help you!"

That's when my house flipping friend said words that warmed my heart. "This isn't an employee…this is our friend!"

The young woman said, "He's family!"

With all of the fuss I made the other day in missing my family during the holidays, I must confess that at that moment, my family was right there by my side. The young couple saw me as a dad, the house flipper as a friend and it was cemented into my heart when after picking out the correct filter.

The young couple looked at me and asked, "Mr. Doug, if you don't have family here in town, we would love for you to spend Thanksgiving with us!" I must tell you that a tear came to my eye at that moment and I couldn't speak. I am such a BABY!

House flipper looked at me and said, "Oh, I like that.. Mr. Doug…is that your name?"

I nodded and she said, "I know my husband's mother is coming from out of town, but he would probably love it if he could talk house renovation with you at the Thanksgiving table!"

I smiled and gained my composure and said, "It is so kind of you both but my wife and I are having a couple of friends over this year…" the young man said, "Well, you sure have helped us…" I got the hug from his wife and he shook my hand and said if we didn't have plans for dessert, they gave me their written address then they left, waving as they walked away.

The house flipping woman finally got all of her questions answered and asked for my last name. I gave it to her and she then packed up her notes and pens and blueprints and off she went into the frigid air.

As I returned to the desk in the flooring department, I took a seat to catch up on follow up with other flooring clients on the computer. At that moment I had a manager on duty come over and said, "Okay…where are they?"

I answered, "Where are what?"

He smiled and said, "the drugs you gave to those customers who just came over and bragged on you?"

I blinked and said, "People are nice…aren't they?"

A long time ago, in a garden far, far away, we all belonged to an unbroken family who enjoyed daily friendship and endless love with one another and our creator. But like the song by *The Sacrifice* Wayne Watson says:

In the land of God's first heartache
When our line of sin began
And the eyes of man were opened
To the evil there at hand
The creator heard the footsteps
But He did not see the man
And God called out for an answer
But He turned away and ran

An attempt in desperation
To be hid from holy eyes
Was to fashion out a garment
That could hide him in disguise

But the Father bled compassion
And with a fast forgiving hand,
Took the life of one yet blameless
And made a covering for the man.

On a hill outside Jerusalem
Where the sin had took its toll
Hung the life of one as blameless
As that garden beast of old,
And He bled with God's compassion
For the evil man had done;
And the heart that cried "Forgive them!"
Was the heart of God's own son."
The broken heart of God's own son.

  I offer to you my friends that we do not recognize each other as brothers and sisters who are far from our garden home because many are still hiding and trying to cover themselves with the leaves of their own making.
  Some are hurt and others…angry.
  But every once in a while, we catch of glimpse of one of our family members and they catch a glimpse of us. For a moment our hearts jump in our chests that we belong to each other, we drift apart again as strangers just like my three friends yesterday.
  It's Thanksgiving season.
  And, our brothers and our sisters are all around us. Some have been found by the Savior, and others refuse to come into the banquet. Whatever we do, let's not give up showing bits of love, and random kindness to our lost family so that; in hope, we will all sit down around the same table holding hands reunited, in a new and living garden from which we will never be cast away again!

A Different Kind of Graduation

When I met Morrie[1], he was a loud-mouthed, foul talking, irresponsible braggart. We were 14 years old and he and I went to school together. He always talked dirty about girls.

Of course, at 14 we didn't know anything about girls, but Morrie said he was experienced. At times he would say things out loud and was cruel with his comments toward them. We all would kind of stand far away from him when he did this…

I was embarrassed.

We went on school field trips and Morrie would always brag about how he could beat up any kid and was mean to the weaker boys in our class. As time went by Morrie was involved in a lot of mischief at school.

He was caught stealing things or sneaking out of school when he was supposed to be in class. I stopped hanging out with him; as did other guys I knew. When we were in High School, Morrie became sullener, and angry.

When the day of graduation came, Morrie gave the peace sign as he walked across the stage and right before he lowered his hands, quickly changed it to flip off the crowd to a few giggles.

Afterward, while families took pictures of their kids, I saw Morrie walking away, pulling off his cap and gown, wadding them up and throwing them in the back of his car. He started the ignition and drove away…and that was the last I saw of him.

Over the years that passed, the memories I had of Morrie were the ones I had from 14-18 years of age. As we all do, I made of lot of judgments about him and resented some of things he did to me and had said to me.

Whenever I would run into classmates and his name was mentioned, none of them would make any comments except to roll their eyes. "He was trouble."

After 20 years I went to my first, class reunion. I had lived too far away to come to the first 2 but at 20 years I finally went. As I arrived; I was so happy to see so many of my old friends.

We caught up about what each of us were doing and I was a little shy about talking to people. I had been pretty outgoing in High School, but I hadn't been the nicest guy either. I spent a lot of time mentioning to people that if I had treated them in bad way that I was sorry. They were all very gracious to me.

I was grateful.

I was tapped on the shoulder by a guy in a nice sport coat and jeans. I turned and said hello. I didn't recognize him. He smiled and said, "It's me, Morrie!" I'm ashamed to say this but I'm sure he could see my face register dread.

I tried my best to smile and make small talk. Morrie smiled again. "It's okay pal, I know I didn't leave people with a very good impression during my school years."

He told me he had been convicted of a few petty crimes and had spent some time in jail. He said it was the most horrendous experience he had ever had.

I listened as he told me of being beat up by a group of men who thought he was a loud-mouth and showed him he wasn't so tough. He said he had to pay $10 a month to a jail hit man to keep him from breaking his arm or leg.

When he got out of jail, he said he had to live in his mother's house until he found a job as a plumber's assistant. He said during his time in jail and on days he was standing knee deep in sewage helping the plumber, he would remember his misspent time in school. How he wished he had done differently but realized his circumstances were due to his poor choices.

****

As time went by, he became certified as a plumber and then a master plumber. He moved to Iowa and began his own business. He met and married a wonderful woman and became a Christian.

When he had heard about the class reunion he decided to come back and ask forgiveness from the people he had wronged. He spent the entire evening going from group to group, person to person, re-introducing himself and asking forgiveness for his poor decisions from school.

One by one, just like me, Morrie won back some respect and as I saw him walk toward his car and drive away…but this time, there was a bounce in his step and a smile on his face. As soon as he left, the chatter was low but it was all about Morrie.

Some said, "I don't believe it…I think he was lying".

Others said, "Wow, what a difference! He is truly a changed man."

But I could tell…just looking in Morrie's eyes, this was a man who had seen the depths of his own soul and met Jesus there.

He was quiet when he spoke, not bragging as in the past and he took care to not exaggerate any of the details. He corrected himself if he felt he had misspoken about something in his story.

As He had turned to leave me that night, he had said, "I should have been a better person and a better friend, and I hope you will forgive me."

I had embraced him and given him a hug. He had a tear in his eye and thanked me for my forgiveness. Morrie didn't make it to the next reunions, and I haven't heard from him since.

I had held Morrie in jail for 20 years before I saw him at that reunion. Lots of things had changed in his life, and I feel badly that I looked crest fallen when I first saw him that night.

But it made me realize how many people we hold in prison in our memories. People can change. People can become completely different over time and even though it's natural to recall someone's bad behavior in the past, realizing that God is active all over the world, we shouldn't be surprised when the Morrie's of our lives show up transformed.

That's Jesus for you.

With everyone he meets, he changes them...the man lying by the pool of Siloam, the woman with the issue of blood, the thief on the cross...and me. If you have done things in your past like me and Morrie and live your life in prison with regret, there is someone waiting in your prison cell who is with you...wanting to change you.

That night, on my way home, I couldn't seem to remember anything that Morrie had done bad in school anymore...it was like God made it all disappear. Somewhere along the way Morrie had gone through another graduation, but his time, his cap and gown were intact, and God was taking pictures…

I'm so proud of you, Morrie!

On That Day...
When the Joy Comes

I've told the story before, but it is worth the telling again of our family trips when I was young. We never really went on vacation as a family; that is to say, to places like Disney World or the Grand Canyon.

We just didn't have the money for that kind of vacation. It was okay though, because we didn't know what we were missing. With four children in the family, we had plenty of entertainment.

My parents, like all parents back in the day, would pull out the old Rand McNally Atlas and once everyone was packed into the car, we would drive to my grandparents' home in Texas.

My father was raised in San Antonio, so making the trek across the country in our family Vista Cruiser from Indiana was quite a journey. Any time we were unsure of which exit to take, my mother (we children called her "Two Lane Lorraine) would pull out the trusty Rand McNally to get our bearings.

****

Fast forward to 2019. These days you can dispense with old Rand and his side kick and dial into your phone the address with zip code of your destination and it will automatically figure your route for you along with gas stations, restaurants and points of interest along the way.

Pretty slick.

Except, there are times when the lady up in space doesn't seem to know where you are. Ever get on the road and she starts saying things like, "turn right at thus and such street..." but your already on Thus and Such street and then she has another glitch and says, "In 500 feet make a U-Turn" but you know you are on the right course?

Somehow, she gets a smack in the head by the satellite and comes back telling you exactly where you are. It can be unnerving if you are out on a deserted country road and she goes on the fritz. You start wish you had two guys named Rand and McNally in the car with you.

In terms of real-life direction navigation, one of the worst things that can happen is to lose sight of your goals. It is said that; in her first attempt to swim the English Channel, Florence Chadwick, due to fog and not being able to see the shore, gave up just 800 yards short of completing her goal.

She was devastated after climbing into the boat to give up and discovering that she had less than a half mile to success! She eventually tried again; this time with clear weather and became the first to successfully swim the channel!

Had she been able to see where she was in relation to the goal, she would never have thrown in the towel. That's what happens when we can't see where we are going. Discouragement sets in, and we begin to feel that the prayer will never be answered, the skill we've practiced for so long will never be mastered or the thing we have been saving for; will never be attained.

Vision along with perseverance are the two oars that enable us to continue rowing when all else tells us to stop. It is particularly important that even if the shoreline; like

Florence Chadwick's, is only in your mind's eye, to keep the goal in sight. I have been on a championship team before; and I can tell you, there were many bumps on the road to the championship.

I wanted to give up many a time!

There were the long practices, the tired, sore muscles, sacrifices that we didn't want to make. At one point, when all of the team was discouraged, our coach would stand up year after year and make the same speech.

You would think he would appeal to individual greatness in each of us…but he did not.

He would say, "You have only one choice…just one." "You can each try to be an individual State Champion OR, you can be a team player and whether you individually capture first place (gymnastics), or not, by doing your best, the whole team can be State Champions."

He was right…and in the years the gymnastics program lasted, we won 13 of 17 State championships.

He knew he needed to show us something tangible to help our flagging vision during the hard times. Each year if our school won the championship, a city firetruck would meet us at the city limits and we would all get on it and ride through the streets of our hometown with the siren blaring.

A banner that read, **STATE CHAMPIONS!**

Our coach, knowing that day was far off in the future for us, would go and purchase a model firetruck and hang it from the ceiling of our locker room with a sign that read…

"Who wants to ride?"

Every day, when we would enter that locker room, that Firetruck hung there, offering us a vision if ours began to fade. I will never forget the faces of even the youngest gymnast on our team…beaming, on the day we saw that fire truck.

It was not cool to cry, but I swear we all were misty eyed, and our coach, stood proudly as we went through the town as champions once again.

****

You may be tired of working so hard for the goal you have of buying a home or saving for the car or vacation. You may have sacrificed for years, saving money to put your children through college.

But Jesus says, "ASK and keep on asking, SEEK and keep on seeking, KNOCK and keep on knocking, for he who asks receives, he who seeks, finds and he who knocks, the door is opened." Matthew 7:7.

Calvin Coolidge said, "Nothing in this world can take the place of persistence. Talent will not: nothing is more common than unsuccessful men with talent. Genius will not; unrewarded genius is almost a proverb. Education will not: the world is full of educated derelicts. Persistence and determination alone are omnipotent."

There are people; many of whom you don't even know, who are cheering for you today. God says there is a great cloud of witness watching as you run your race. I encourage you my friend, don't give up. You may have had some real low points in your life and maybe it seems your best days are behind you…they are not! Jeremiah 33: says:

"Call to me, and I will show you great and mighty things which you do not know" God isn't mad at you. He won't give up. His love never stops. He doesn't say, "That's it! I've

HAD it with you!" God never blows his stack…never. Keep asking, keep seeking and keep knocking…because the day is coming when the fog is going to clear and you are going to see the shoreline!! The day is going to arrive when you see the firetruck…and all of the hard work and all of the sacrifice will melt away… on that day, when the joy comes."

[i] https://www.desiringgod.org/articles/interruption-is-gods-invitation

[ii] https://www.mnn.com/lifestyle/arts-culture/stories/10-famous-people-who-died-before-they-were-household-names

[iii] Ibid

[iv] Ibid

[v] Ibid

[vi] Ibid

[vii] Ibid

[viii] https://www.hrc.utexas.edu/educator/modules/gutenberg/johann/

[ix] https://videosift.com/he-West-Wing-Josh-Lyman-and-Men-on-Mars

Doug Pacheco is a writer, speaker and storyteller who is passionate about recognizing opportunities and taking advantage of them in order to share the love of Jesus with others. He is a former pastor and missionary. Doug writes a daily blog at unremarkablemiracles.com. He resides near Nashville Tennessee with his wife Mary Ann.

Milton Keynes UK
Ingram Content Group UK Ltd.
UKHW021813280823
427632UK00010B/1273